I Send You Your ANGEL GABRIEL

A Family's Journey Through Faith

Antonietta Bommino

G.A. PRESS

G.A.Press
2984 State Street
Carlsbad, CA 92008

Designed by Mary Embree

Jacket design by Abacus Graphics

Library of Congress Catalog Card Number: 98-093874

ISBN: 0-9664510-0-7

Printed in the United States of America

Contents

Dedication
Acknowledgments

Dedication

This book is dedicated to God, Our Father who encouraged me to write about all the wonderful things He has done for me and my family throughout these years. Today I continue to see the amazing things He does in our lives. I thank you, my God, for loving me unconditionally. May this book be filled with Your love, the love You've shown me all these years. I love You, my Lord, my God, and I thank You.

Secondly, to my Mother Mary in heaven. You touched my heart when I was a youngster at Lourdes, and you took a piece of my heart with you. Thank you, my precious lady, queen of all the angels, until we meet.

Thirdly, to my daughter Gabriella who truly opened our eyes in life to see where our Lord Jesus Christ wanted us. We thank you, our sweet angel, for the joy you brought us. Even though it was a short time, it was eternity for us. We'll never forget your soul. Rest in peace with all the angels and saints and at the side of our Lord Jesus Christ in heaven. Protect us all and be our Guardian Angel Gabriella.

Acknowledgments

I want to thank my husband, who guided me through each and every day. You've been my rock. A piece of His rock. A strong and sturdy one. I love you for who you are and all you do. I thank God for you and your love for Him.

To my sons, may God's blessing be with you both. May He keep you on that narrow path. Keep your eyes on Him, and you'll never go wrong.

Luigi, you are our miracle in life. You've taught us how to believe, and to get up every time we fall. We love you, Luigi.

Gianluca, you are the joy in our life. You brought us happiness in the time we needed it the most. You were there to fill the emptiness in our hearts. We love you, Gianluca.

To my whole family: Mom, Dad, Mary, Elena, Tony, Zio Carlo and Zia Carmela, who are always there in times of need, happy or sad. And to my friends. I thank God for you all. May our love for each other grow more and more each day. And may we continue to be there for each other. I love you and thank you all.

But the Lord stood at my side

and gave me strength...

2 Timothy 4:17-18

CHAPTER ONE

The Beginning

In Him we were also chosen, having been pre-
destined according to the plan of Him who works
out everything in conformity with the purpose of
His will.

~Ephesians 1:11

As one part of my life was coming to an end, a new beginning was about take place—my life was about to take a turn. In June of 1977 I graduated from Rolling Hills High School in Southern California. That summer my family went to Italy on vacation. We spent a month in Southern Italy. The water was crystal clear, the air was warm and the people were great. Most of our time was spent at the most beautiful resort around, my uncle's hotel and restaurant called "California Beach." Our window overlooked the spectacular waters of the Mediterranean Sea. Beauty filled our eyes everywhere we turned. This paradise is called Marina

Di Pulsano. Both my parents were born and raised in this area, and during our stay we spent a great deal of time with all our relatives.

While we were staying at the resort, my Uncle Frank assigned a waiter to take care of the family table each time we were to dine. A young man named Luigi, nicknamed Gino, was to help out with the family's meals. He was a polite young man with a radiant smile and eyes the color of the sea. He didn't speak much but he was always nearby. We never had to look far for him.

Gino finally began to say a few words to me, always complimenting me. I didn't pay much attention to him because I wasn't really interested at the time. I had a boyfriend whom I had been going with for three years, all through high school.

It was two weeks before our trip was to be over and my parents wanted my sisters and me to see other parts of Italy and Europe. My Uncle drove us through Venice, Pisa, and Geneva. The waters were indescribable. The cities were like pictures from history books, come to life. What exquisite sights. Full of love, that country is! We took a train from Geneva to southern France; our destination was the city of Lourdes.

The train passed through *La Costa Azura*, "the Blue Coast." I've seen many beautiful places, but this ride put all the others to shame. When we arrived the train let us off right in the center of the city of Lourdes and we jumped off the train and walked to the area all visitors go, to see where St. Bernadette saw "Our Lady."

There were thousands and thousands of people there! They wheeled the sick in by the hundreds. Wheelchairs, hospital beds, crutches. Ailing people were all around us. I remember as we got closer to the entrance there was a large black iron gate and a driveway of asphalt that sloped downward. As we walked down we could see the glorious statue of Our Lady. There were hundreds of blooming flowers below her. It was awe inspiring. I stared at her for a long while. I couldn't believe what I was seeing.

As we turned to our right facing the statue, we saw a stone fence and a small cobblestone road that led to St. Bernadette's house. To the left of the statue is a walkway that leads to the area where a large altar has been made to hold many masses. It sits in a grotto. Facing the altar, one can walk up to the area where Our Lady told Bernadette to dig a well. But there was only dirt there then. Later on, after the townspeople had laughed at her for getting mud on her face, she wasn't sure what Our Lady was really asking of her. As she was being taken away from the location, a young man saw the water begin to run from the hole she had dug. That same hole still stands there today. Many are still being healed in its blessed waters.

There is an area where people line up to take baths in the waters for healing. At the time I didn't think much about the healing waters. But my mother and older sister did go in. Inside there were many Roman tubs with shower curtains dividing them. My sister was taken to one and my mother to another. Mom went in first. The water was cold and Mom was concerned for my sister who had been very sick that year. She told the nun the water was too cold for her daughter.

"*Signora*, how little faith you have," the nun said.

Mom stepped in only to find that the water turned warm once she was in it. It was like magic.

When later she and my sister were to step out of the water they found that there were no towels.

Mom said, "Sister, my daughter, she needs a towel, she might get sick."

The nun again said "*Signora*, still you have so little faith."

By the time they stopped talking, got dressed, and walked out, my mother and sister were completely dry.

No matter what we're shown in life, we still tend to doubt our faith. We need to keep our faith strong. As Jesus said in Matthew 17:20, *"Because you have so little faith I tell you the truth, if you have faith as small as a mustard seed, you can say to this mountain, move from here to there and it will move. Nothing will be impossible for you."*

As we were leaving the area we saw people filling bottles, vases, anything that would hold water. It was the water from the grotto where Our Lady appeared to Bernadette on February 11, 1858. On top of the grotto are all the stations of the cross in the most elaborate art work imaginable. It's something that all who believe should go and see. To this day I remember it in detail. It's still fresh in my mind.

One day soon, with God's blessing and grace, I hope to take my family to Lourdes, so they can understand and experience what I did that summer in 1977. I truly believe that Our Lady of Lourdes kept a part of my heart when I left there.

After we left Lourdes we went back to Italy, touring

some more on our way south. When we returned we learned that Gino was supposed to go on a trip to Venice with his friends. So Gino and I said our good-byes because I was to leave for America at the end of the week.

All was well. But I felt sad that he was leaving. Was I starting to like him a little too much?

A few hours went by, and Gino showed up again. We all wondered why he was there; even his friends couldn't understand. Well, it turned out Gino was in love—in love with me. How could this be? Well guess what? We can't change what God has planned for us.

We had gotten to know each other a little. Although he understood that I had a boyfriend and he respected that, he was still determined that he was going to be my husband. He went home to tell his parents that he was going to marry the American girl. His parents thought he was crazy. But the day before we left, he had his parents come down to the resort to meet me. My mother told them that she wasn't going to interfere but she wanted them to know that I was pretty serious about a young man named Robert back home.

By this time I was very confused. I wasn't sure what was happening to me. I felt sad about leaving, but I was going home to my boyfriend. As the days and weeks went by, I'd pray, "Dear God, what do I do? I'm so confused." I'd cry endless nights, wondering what was best for me. Finally I decided that I wanted Gino. But many times I felt scared. Would my life with Robert or Gino be better? Oh, my God, what do I do? But God knew exactly what I was going to do. He had written everything about my life before I was born.

For two months after we left Italy, Gino continued to send me registered letters. And every Sunday, faithfully, he called. We'd talk for awhile and then our parents would speak with each other. On November 4, 1977, Gino flew to California. I met him at Los Angeles International airport and we drove to Palm Springs where my family and I were living after I graduated. As we sat at the dinner table with the whole family around us, he pulled a ring out of his pocket.

"What is this for?" Mom asked him.

"I came to marry your daughter, *Signora*," Gino replied. "I didn't come to visit America."

The room was silent; things were happening fast.

On March 5, 1978, we were married at St. Peter's Italian Catholic Church in Los Angeles, with 500 guests at the wedding. The ceremony was said in Italian and English. My response was in English, Gino's in Italian. It was a night to remember for a lifetime.

It's amazing how our lives can change literally overnight. One day things are going along just fine and you have your life all planned, but if it's not God's plan for you, He will change it.

In May of 1978, two months after Gino and I were married, Gino's mother passed away. Gino was devastated. His mother was his joy. We weren't able to go to Italy because we were getting Gino's papers together. He was an Italian citizen and his visa had expired. So we planned a trip to Italy in June, once all was done with his documents.

We knew his dad was very sick but we never expected what we saw when we arrived. The large, healthy man that he was had become a fragile little person. He was diagnosed with cancer of the liver. It was no surprise to him, he said, for he had told his wife he'd be with her within a month.

During the time we spent together he managed to have a few good days and he told me how much he and my mother-in-law loved me. He asked me to watch over his son and stay close to him always. Shortly after that, early one morning while we were all asleep, Dad went home, home to heaven with Our Father. Home, to be with his wife. As he felt that he couldn't survive without her, he prayed for his death to be a fast one and God had answered his prayer.

While we were in Italy we took care of Dad's things.

We thank God that Gino and I were able to see his father before he was gone. I am grateful for that special afternoon when Gino brought his parents to meet me, for that was the only opportunity I ever had to share precious time with both his mother and father together.

Life continued for us. We were your normal kind of couple. We worked, enjoyed our life together, and then one day we received the happy news that we were expecting.

CHAPTER TWO

A Mother's Nightmare

For nothing is impossible with God.
~Luke 1:37

My labor and delivery were not easy by any means, although I did deliver our firstborn naturally. I had gone through severe back labor. I thought the pain would never end. Finally, on August 17, 1979, after twelve hours of labor, our baby arrived.

As soon as our baby was born, I noticed that there was a lot of commotion going on in the delivery room, but no one was letting me know what was happening. I heard the public address system calling for a pulmonary specialist, "code blue." I was lying right there, yet no one gave me any indication that something was wrong with our child. While the doctors and nurses huddled around our newborn, I was left unattended for some time. Finally, the doctor took care of me and I was taken to my room.

I felt that something was wrong but I wasn't sure what was happening. Was this all normal? Was our child okay? When would I know if our baby was a boy or a girl?

Later, when I was settled in my room and began to have my meal, the doctor came in and told Gino and me about some problems our child had at birth. I can remember feeling a knot in my stomach. The doctor explained that the baby had a collapsed lung and needed to be on a respirator and oxygen. He needed help to breathe. Also, the child was born with an omphalocele—an umbilical hernia which causes the intestine to be on the outside of the stomach wall.

I interrupted him and asked, "Do we have a boy or girl?" Not that it was the most important thing at that moment, but I wanted to know.

"It's a boy!" the doctor answered.

Now the baby had a name: Luigi Amedeo Bommino. Hours went by before I could see my son. At last they brought him into my room in an incubator. He had tubes hooked up to him and his little tummy was all bandaged in white gauze. We were able to touch him, but only through holes on the sides of the incubator. I wanted to hold him and caress him. He was our creation, our gift from heaven, but why was this all happening? What did I do wrong during my pregnancy? I tried to go back and remember what I ate and drank. My husband reassured me that it wasn't my fault this was happening, that I never smoked or drank alcohol or took any medications. But that wasn't enough. Why our child? Was this a punishment from God? We had prayed for nine months and tried to maintain our peace of mind. Did I not do something that I was supposed to have done? I just didn't know anymore.

It's a mother's nightmare to deliver a child who has medical complications. We wanted to know how long before we could take our baby home. Some said one month, others just didn't know.

Shortly after he was born, Luigi was on his way to Loma Linda University Hospital, about a fifty-minute drive from where we were. There they could treat him for his birth problems. Desert Hospital in Palm Springs was not equipped for these types of birth problems.

While I was left alone at Desert Hospital, Luigi was transported by ambulance to Loma Linda and my husband followed. I felt I couldn't stay one more hour in that room, hearing the other babies around me and sensing so much happiness in the air. I wasn't a part of the joy. I was to be different. I asked if I could be discharged and the doctors agreed only if I promised to go home and rest for twenty-four hours.

"Sure. No problem," I said. But when my mother picked me up I asked her to drive me to Loma Linda University Hospital to be with my baby and my husband.

The drive was a very quiet and lonely one. The unknown was eating me alive! Finally we arrived and went up to Pediatrics Critical Care.

Luigi was a very sick little boy. He had the respirator for breathing taped to his mouth and IVs and tubes all over. I could hardly see his face or body. It was the most painful experience parents could ever go through, looking at their child under these circumstances.

We stayed at Loma Linda several days. On the third day they took Luigi in to surgery for heart catheterization. They said they needed to explore more around the heart area. So, only three days old, Luigi was on his way to his first surgery.

Gino, Mom and I were in the hospital waiting room

when I began to feel very sick. I started to bleed quite heavily. Not knowing what to expect after having my first child, I thought it was normal. Finally I asked Mom if I should be bleeding as much as I was.

Mom was concerned, so we went down to the emergency room in the hospital. But as the wait was to be an hour and a half, we decided to drive back to Palm Springs and see my obstetrician. We called him, and he said to meet us in his office. I had to leave while my baby was in surgery, but my husband stayed behind with him.

By that time the bleeding had become uncontrollable and I was hemorrhaging. We arrived at the doctor's office after hours and the doctor and his nurse, who was also his wife, were waiting for us. I explained what was going on and he had me go into another room and change. After talking with me he decided to do a D and C, a dilation and curettage—scraping the inside of the uterus. Right there and right then! No medication, no anesthesia. I still remember the pain vividly, of bursting into a cold sweat and clawing the walls with my fingernails. It was worse than the delivery itself.

When it was over he had removed a large portion of placenta left over from the delivery of Luigi. Because

Luigi had needed so much attention I had been left without being cleaned out after his birth. Thank God that was over.

Again I was told to go home and stay off of my feet for twenty-four hours. Easy for them to say; it wasn't their child in the hospital having surgery at that very moment. My mother became very firm about taking me home to rest. She felt she already had a grandson in intensive care and did not want her daughter there too! So we went home.

But I couldn't get much rest. My mind and heart were with my husband and son at the hospital. At last the surgery was over. Luigi did well, but he was still a very sick newborn.

As the weeks went by, he wasn't improving much. By the third week a decision had to be made to give him a tracheotomy, to make an opening in his throat for breathing. He was fighting the respirator too much. It was the best decision for him. We were looking at another month at least, they said, before we could think about taking him home.

The "trac" surgery was successful, and now the doctors wanted to do his first abdominal surgery, to attempt to push his intestine into the abdominal cavity. They said that Luigi's omphalocele was one of the largest they had seen. It is a very rare birth defect that occurs in the first stages of pregnancy and is usually fatal.

Luigi's lungs were immature even though he was full term. One of the upper lobe walls was collapsed and he couldn't breath on his own. Off he went to surgery again, but this time it was different. While the doctors were trying to slowly roll the large sac of organs into his stomach cavity, Luigi went into cardiac arrest, so they stopped. Many surgeries followed without success.

The doctors decided to try adding animal skin to the top of his intestines and try to roll them in little by little. Again Luigi's breathing would not cooperate with the procedure. The final decision was to wrap his tummy tightly with an Ace bandage so his body would accept the changes. (The defect caused his diaphragm to drop very low to his tummy.) Little by little the bandage was tightened for days at a time.

We'd often receive a call about Luigi in the middle of the night. We went through many nights rushing to the hospital and wondering if we would get there in time, knowing the drive would take at least an hour.

Where was God when we needed Him? Where was He to help our son? Why couldn't a miracle take place?

CHAPTER THREE

Our First Encounter

An angel from Heaven appeared to him and strengthened him.

~Luke 22/43

When Luigi was about three months old, we received a phone call at two in the morning from the hospital. We were told to come immediately because he wasn't doing well. So my mother, my husband and I rushed down from Palm Springs.

When we arrived things weren't looking good at all and we knew we had to get Luigi baptized and anointed. When we asked where we could find a priest, we were told that Loma Linda Hospital was of the Seventh Day Adventist faith and there weren't any priests there. The nearest place to find one would be in Redlands, about fifteen minutes away. The head nurse said there was a chapel downstairs if we wanted to pray. We knew we might not have time to go all the way to Redlands to find a priest but we weren't convinced that there wasn't anyone there who could bless and baptize our son.

We frantically searched for a phone book to find a local priest. We got into the elevator knowing that time was against us. We arrived at the lobby and, as the doors opened, there stood a tall, well-groomed gentleman with a white collar, holding a Bible.

He looked at us and asked, "Bommino family?"

"Yes," we answered.

We never exited the elevator but headed right back up to the ward where our son was. The priest went into Luigi's room and we were asked to wait outside. Luigi had gone into cardiac arrest and the staff was all around him trying to revive him. The doctor in the room finally gave up saying there wasn't anything more to be done. At that same time, the priest was anointing and blessing Luigi. The respiratory therapist, however, never gave up. She continued to ventilate him by way of the tracheostomy.

A while had passed and my husband made his way into the room. At that moment, Luigi began to cough. The staff and doctor ran back in to assist him and things got back on track. When Gino turned to thank the priest, he was nowhere to be seen. Gino ran out and asked the nurses where the tall gentleman had gone, but they only looked at us as though we were crazy. They again told us that there were no priests in the hospital and that there surely wasn't a priest there that morning.

Well, we knew better. We saw him, he spoke to us, we walked with him up to the room. Gino took off running toward the elevator to find the priest, to thank him and to give him an offering. But no luck. He was nowhere to be found. Gino continued to run to the parking lot, only to find no one. No sight of anybody, anywhere.

As we went into Luigi's room we knew in our hearts that someone had been there. The nurses were still looking at us strangely, but we knew someone had anointed and blessed our son and saved him from death. On Luigi's forehead was Holy Oil. The Lord had sent us His angel to baptize and anoint our son.

Luigi was later transferred to Children's Hospital in Los Angeles, where he remained in the Intensive Care Unit until he was nineteen months old, never to experience the warm sun on his face or the cool wind through his hair.

Finally, God granted us the gift of life and sent Luigi home. There we had a long road ahead of us—doctor appointments, surgeries, home nursing care twenty-four hours a day, the tracheostomy, oxygen, and a gastrostomy for his feedings—for the next several years.

As our son grew older his problems minimized. During those years we almost lost him on many occasions. But the Lord was always by his side. He continued to spare his life. Our Lord kept guiding us through all our deepest valleys and helped us get to the other side each time.

CHAPTER FOUR

Our Little Angel Arrives

In this you greatly rejoice, though now for a little while you may have had to suffer grief in all kinds of trials.

~I Peter 1:6

The years went by and Gino and I decided we wanted to have another child. But it was not going to be easy. In 1988 alone I had five miscarriages. But the Lord finally blessed us.

I was about four months into my pregnancy and all was going well. We couldn't wait to find out what we were going to have. It was a Monday evening and I had gone upstairs to bed. Luigi and his cousin Alexandria were in Luigi's room and my husband was downstairs. I was sleeping when I felt the presence of a man. I could tell that someone was there in the room.

Then I heard a voice say to me, "I'm sending you your Angel Gabriel."

After the words were spoken the man touched me. I could feel his large but gentle hand on my right shoulder. I screamed. But when I opened my eyes, there wasn't anybody there.

Luigi and Alexandria came running into the room and my husband ran upstairs. They all wanted to know what was going on. I asked my son if he or Alexandria had been in my room. Neither one had; they had both been in his room playing Nintendo. My husband had been downstairs watching television. So who was it who came into my room to speak to me and touch my shoulder?

I explained to them what had happened and they were all in awe. Gino and I spoke about it for a while, full of joy. I knew then that God had granted me a little girl.

Three weeks went by and we hadn't thought about that Monday night very much. When I went for an ultrasound exam I found out that, sure enough, it was a girl. The Lord had once again sent a messenger to let us know.

I remember the joy we felt after the ultrasound was taken. Our smiles were from ear to ear. As we left the doctor's office we were jumping and laughing; joy filled our hearts completely. I recall saying to Gino, "If anybody is watching us they'll think we're crazy." But we didn't care what anyone thought. We were having our little girl.

For the next five months everything went well as we waited for the blessed event. And on July 2, 1990, our Lord delivered safely to us our little angel. She was beautiful.

From the time she arrived into this world, she touched our hearts and we knew exactly what her name was going to be. Gabriella Angelina Gracia, Angel Gabriel! I had been told during my visit from God's messenger that that was who he was sending, and so that was the name we gave her. July 2 is also the Madonna Di Gracia's day, the day of our Lady of Grace. She is our mother and mother of all, so we chose to use her name as well. Being Catholic and Italian, we strongly believe in our saint's days and Blessed days.

The days, the months, and then a year went by. Our beautiful baby became a beautiful little girl, a special gift from heaven. She was very healthy, full of life and joy, always smiling, always happy. She would turn heads no matter where I was with her. But it wasn't the regular "Oh, how cute" or "How beautiful." It was something that touched anyone who had eye contact with her. Her eyes would enter part of your heart. Her beauty was an inner beauty as well as an outer beauty. People would tell me that her eyes sparkled like the stars in heaven. Strangers as well as family said the same thing—there's something very special about her eyes, her look—this is a special child. Of course, as parents we thought the same, never thinking that she could really be an angel sent from heaven.

In the spring of 1991 my mother, my son, my daughter and I had the pleasure of spending a month and a half in Italy. Gabriella had her first birthday there. It had been fifteen years since either my husband or I had been back to Italy. It was definitely an unplanned trip but, of course, planned in the Lord's eyes. All my family members and my husband's family were able to see our children.

What a blessed gift to all of us. Luigi, who they thought they would probably never see due to all of his illnesses, was there to enjoy their love and company, and Gabriella, the new addition to the family. The Lord surely has planned each and every one of our lives for us, no doubt about that. He had managed not only the unexpected trip for us, but the togetherness of family, the unity, the love. Our families in Italy would never have known Gabriella if it hadn't been for the grace of God. He let them experience a little of heaven through Gabriella.

We had an enjoyable visit and we will always have the memories of that special trip. Although it was to have been only for a month, we managed to extend the visit for two more weeks.

We returned home on July 7. It had been so long since we had seen Gino and we had so much to share that we went on and on for days about our trip.

CHAPTER FIVE

Gianluca Joins the Family

He will be a joy and delight to you, and many will rejoice because of his birth, for he will be great in the sight of the Lord.

~Luke 1:17

Surprise, surprise! A few weeks after we return from Italy I find that I am pregnant again. On April 7, 1992, our third child, Gianluca Vincenzo, was born. Strong, big, and full of spirit. What a blessing he was. We wondered why we were sent this child, since it wasn't planned, but it was in God's plans. He was a healthy 9 pounds, 2 ounces. The delivery was my most difficult, he was just too big. After twelve hours of labor and one hour of delivery Gianluca finally arrived.

Again, it seemed that all was well. We couldn't ask for more from our lives. We loved each other. Luigi, our eldest, had been doing very well, no problems. Gabriella was almost two years old and Gianluca was growing like a weed. Then one morning while we were having coffee, Gino was holding Gianluca and playing with him when he noticed a large golf ball-sized lump on his neck near his jugular vein. In a panic, Gino yelled and asked me if I had noticed this lump before. I was sure that the lump had never been there. I had bathed him, breast-fed him, and had never seen it. It definitely was something new.

We called our doctor immediately and were told to bring him in to the office right away. Scared to death the whole drive there, we didn't want to think the worst. After the doctor had seen Gianluca, he assured us that it was nothing serious. He diagnosed it as torticollis, a strained muscle due to hard labor. It is a symptom that shows up about a month after a difficult delivery. And Gianluca was about four weeks old by now. But, he said, let's have a specialist look at it to be sure.

So off we went to see a throat specialist. He ordered ultrasound x-rays, and everything came back negative. His next suggestion was to do a biopsy by removing fluid or tissue from the lump and having it sent to the laboratory for testing. There we were with a perfectly healthy son, and this doctor had to stick a large needle into his throat. I can remember the hurt and the pain. It felt as though I was getting that needle stuck in me. Finally it was done, and I can remember just squeezing him and loving him and praying, Oh, please, Lord, don't let it be cancer or a tumor.

Another day went by, and we received a phone call from the surgeon:

"Well, we don't know what's there. We'll have to go on in and see what it is," he said.

Although we reminded him of the pediatrician's diagnosis, he chose to go ahead and operate. If there was something there, it would be removed and tested; if not, at least we would know it was nothing. Gino and I looked at each other, thinking out loud, "Well, he's the specialist."

Another two weeks of hell went by, appointment after appointment. On a Friday afternoon we decided to go ahead with the surgery. But as the weekend came upon us, we didn't feel comfortable with the surgeon's decision. The more we thought about it, the more we didn't like it. On Sunday morning Gino said he had decided that Gianluca needed a second opinion. So we called Dr. Hansen, Luigi's surgeon at Children's Hospital in Los Angeles.

Dr. Hansen had saved our son Luigi's life time after time. We had all the confidence in the world in him.

When we finally reached him, he assured us that it sounded like Gianluca had what is called torticollis. There was that word again. After I described the delivery to him, he had no doubt about it.

He said over the phone, "I'm sure that's what it is. If I'm wrong, it will be one out of a million!"

Gino asked, "How can you be so sure if the surgeon here has seen him and has all of the tests in front of him, yet he still wants to operate?"

Dr. Hansen didn't have an answer, but again he assured us that Gianluca was fine. He said this usually goes away in two to four weeks and never comes back. He also said that since we were going to bring Luigi in for a preoperative appointment on the coming Wednesday, we should bring Gianluca in and he would look at him just to make sure. Luigi had been having some stomach problems and through an ultrasound a gallstone was found in his gallbladder. Dr. Hansen was to do the surgery.

Gabriella stayed at my Aunt Carmela's house with my mom and family, and we left for Thousand Oaks where Dr. Hansen's office was. The ride took about three and a half hours from our house in Vista, near San Diego. When we finally arrived Dr. Hansen first checked Luigi out, okayed him for surgery, and then took a look at Gianluca.

It was not surprising to him that his diagnosis by phone was correct.

Gino again asked, "But how can you be sure? You didn't look at the x-rays or the MRI."

Dr. Hansen assured us that there was nothing to worry about but that he would have his radiologist read the x-rays and MRI and get back to us the next day.

Gino asked, "Doctor, how can you give a diagnosis over the phone and be correct while another doctor who has all the tests in front of him still can't see it?"

"It's like a good mechanic and a bad one," Dr. Hansen replied. "One can just listen to the problem and, through experience, know what's wrong, while the other one has to take the car apart to find out what's going on."

He needed to say no more, our hearts were at peace.

As soon as we left the office we picked up the car phone. The whole family was waiting for our call. We were able to tell them that God had laid His hands over Gianluca and saved him from any illness. And that Luigi's gallbladder surgery was scheduled for July 10.

On our way home Luigi, with such confidence, said, "I knew he would be okay. Look at me. I'm a walking miracle."

In three weeks the lump was completely gone. We returned to Dr. Hansen's office to be sure things were going well. And, sure enough, God's healing was at work again.

CHAPTER SIX

A Very Sick Little Girl

Even though my illness was a trial to you, you did not treat me with contempt or scorn. Instead you welcomed me as if I were an angel of God.
~Galatians 4:14

A few days had passed, and Gabriella was sitting on her father's lap. A little "daddy's girl," she did that a lot. She was in his arms watching television when all of a sudden she turned and stared so deeply into his eyes that it scared him.

"Gabriella, *a papa*," Gino asked her, "what do you want to tell me? Why are you looking at me like this?"

It seemed as though she were in a trance, communicating with someone through her father's eyes. Then she came out of the trance and became alert again. That evening Gino said he was very concerned about what had happened. He felt that her "spacing out" was not normal, that she had never done that before.

In our hearts today we understand that the Lord was preparing her for what lay ahead for her and for us. Through her earthly father's eyes she was listening to her eternal Father's words.

During the following month, Gabriella was in and out of the pediatrician's office several times, the doctor never really pinpointing anything wrong. We thought it might be flu symptoms. She wasn't eating well but we associated her loss of appetite with her age and normal changes in eating patterns. Still, she just wasn't looking right. She seemed fragile and pale and didn't have as much energy as she normally had. In my heart I wasn't fully content with the diagnosis that there was nothing wrong.

Around the middle of May, Gabriella got a "hurt" between her toes. It would get better, then it would get worse. It just wouldn't heal and then it began to look infected. Also, a lump in her groin area had enlarged and the doctor thought it was related to the infection in her foot. So back on antibiotics she went. During that same time we noticed that she would trip a lot; she seemed clumsy. Not knowing what was really going on, we would chuckle because it would happen so often.

When she had her eighteen-month health check, all

was well. There were no signs of an illness developing.

In June my sisters and I planned to spend a few days in Las Vegas. I needed a little break from the trauma we had gone through with Gianluca. So I loaded up the Blazer and off we went. Gabriella was jumping up and down, being the active little girl that she was.

But after awhile she seemed to become very uncomfortable. Suddenly, she let out a loud scream and then began to cry. I had to pull over to see what was wrong. I took her out of her car seat and let her stretch. Then I changed her diaper and off we went again. When we arrived at my sister's house in Mission Lakes she began to play with her cousin Sabrina. When she took her shirt off to play in the little pool outside, my sister Mary noticed that Gabriella's abdomen seemed very swollen. I told her we had been back and forth to the doctors and nothing was wrong. But she wasn't satisfied with that. Gabriella's spine and abdomen were distended.

As evening arrived, Gabriella became chilled off and on and her color wasn't good; her lips were blue. It was the middle of the night before she finally got to sleep. The next morning her temperature was up to 104.8 degrees and there was nothing I could do to get it down. Shortly afterward, she began vomiting bile and I knew something was seriously wrong with her.

At 9 a.m. we called my sister's pediatrician. When we told him Gabriella's symptoms, he advised us to bring her in right away. I called our doctor and he agreed that she needed to be seen. We drove to Palm Springs where the doctor's office was, and she was checked over. Her body by this time was limp and she was almost comatose.

As I was leaving to take Gabriella to the lab for tests, the doctor commented, "I want you to know it could be mononucleosis, hepatitis, or something else."

I carried her into the laboratory and the young lady there asked me if she was on her way to the hospital. I remember getting a little defensive. I responded, "No, she's only getting x-rays and lab work."

The girl replied, "I'm sorry, she looks so sick and the doctor ordered so many tests." After the tests we went to my mother's house to wait for the results.

Hours went by with no word, so around 2 p.m. I phoned and asked for the results. The nurse had been calling my sister's house for hours, thinking that we were there. When she told me that the doctor wanted to see me, I knew there was something seriously wrong. I remember asking if he wanted me to bring Gabriella.

The nurse said, "Absolutely. Doctor Lewis wants to see her immediately."

I looked at my mom and said, "Something bad is wrong with my daughter."

My heart was torn apart, not knowing what was in store for her. I only knew she was very sick.

My sister had stepped out for a moment and was not back yet so I had to drive to the doctor's office alone with Gabriella. Mom stayed with Gianluca. When we arrived, Gabriella was vomiting. Oh, how sick she was. I carried her in and sat down with her to wait for the doctor.

I prayed, Please, God, don't let it be AIDS, or leukemia, or cancer. I kept saying those words again and again. It was as if the Lord had already laid them on my heart.

When Dr. Lewis came in he said, "Your sister and I have been friends for a long time now and that makes what I have to say particularly hard. I don't know how else to tell you this except to come straight to the point. Your daughter has leukemia."

I remember pulling Gabriella close to my heart and screaming, "Oh God, no!"

I felt as though my whole life had crumbled before

me. I could only think of death at that moment. The only thing I had ever heard about leukemia was that it was a terrible illness, that death usually followed. My angel, my joy, my child would eventually die.

We had waited so long for her, why was God taking her now? Why did He give her to us just to take her back? Why does this have to happen to us? What have we done to deserve this? Why this? Why us? Haven't we gone through enough already? I was mad at God!

Dr. Lewis kept asking me all kinds of questions, but my mind was blank. I could only feel the loss already. She was my princess; all I'd dreamed of and she was going to be taken from me.

Unless someone has experienced something like this, they can't imagine the pain a mother feels knowing that her child is going to die. The helplessness, the fear, the anger. The pull in your heart as it's tearing apart. You just want to crawl into a hole and die. I had asked the Lord to spare this pain, this illness, this disease. I had asked Him to grant me one more miracle. He's always been with us. Why did I feel so abandoned at this time?

It was time to decide if we wanted Gabriella to be life-flighted to Children's Hospital in Los Angeles or in San

Diego. It had just hit me that my husband still knew nothing about this! I panicked. I had to page him. How was I going to tell him that his princess was going to die? Just then my sisters came into the room. We hugged, we cried and we screamed together. We were helpless! At last the phone rang, and it was Gino. The doctor asked if I wanted to tell my husband, or did I want him to tell him. I chose to tell him myself.

"Gabriella is really sick," I said.

He asked, "What is it?"

"She has leukemia."

He couldn't understand. I told him several times. Finally I told him in Italian. Then he realized what it was. His yells and screams were unbelievable.

"Are you sure?" he asked. "Let me talk to the doctor."

Before giving the phone to the doctor I said to Gino, "Do you understand what she has? Our baby is going to die!"

Dr. Lewis spoke with him to get his okay to transfer Gabriella to Children's Hospital in San Diego. We decided on San Diego because it was closer to our home and it might be a long-term stay.

We drove her to Desert Hospital Emergency. There

she was "prepped" and made ready for the transfer. She was so sick, she was slipping in and out of a slight coma. Her white blood cell count was at 650,000; a count of 10,000 is normal. The cancer had taken over most of her good red cells.

Watching the helicopter lifting up, I could only pray to my God that He would protect her from this awful cancer and give her back to me as she was before. Gino and our dear friend Johnny waited at Children's Hospital for her arrival. As he waited, Gino could only envision her kissing him and jumping into the Blazer, the way she was when we left the day before. How things had changed in twenty-four hours. Our life was like a movie on a big screen. I thought these things happened only on television. But no, this was reality and definitely no movie. It was our life and our problem.

Gabriella was on her way to Children's Hospital while I had to go back to my mom's house, pick up her and Gianluca, and head out to Vista. Not much was said as I was driving. My sight was so blurry from the tears that kept welling up in my eyes that I couldn't see the road. Mom suggested that I pull over and let her drive. While I was sitting there in a daze, questions kept coming to my mind. Oh dear God, are You going to save my child? How long do we have before she dies? Was there any cure for this type of leukemia?

The questions kept rolling around in my head, but there were no answers yet. We finally arrived in Vista, dropped Gianluca off at my Aunt Carmela's house, and got back on the road to Children's Hospital. Two and a half hours had gone by since I'd been with my daughter and I still had another forty-five-minute drive ahead.

In the meantime Gabriella arrived at Children's Hospital where her dad and Johnny met her. The tears, the pain they both felt was indescribable. When we finally arrived, Gino was in a meeting with Dr. Spruce, the hematologist and oncologist. He had begun to explain the whole picture to Gino. When I walked in I could only hold my husband and cry. I could feel his pain because it was going right through me.

Gabriella was admitted to the intensive care unit in very critical condition. Dr. Spruce explained to us that AMML was a very rare form of leukemia and that they had some chemotherapy they could try. But first things first. We had to make sure Gabriella made it through the next five days in the ICU, which at this point was not looking very good. The main thing was to get her white cell count down so they could start the chemotherapy.

They began to "wash" her blood and then give it back to her. They repeated it five times before any chemotherapy was given. We never left her side. All during the night we prayed, crying and wondering what the future held for us. Why was this happening? How was it going to end?

Now it was Day Two. We had called our pastor, Doug Regan, and he came right away. Not much was said. He could tell that things weren't looking good. We stood around Gabriella's bedside in the ICU room, Mom, Father Doug, Gino and I. Father Doug began to pray. The prayer was silent but powerful. The Spirit fell upon Gabriella so strongly. Father Doug prayed from the top of her head and worked his way down to her feet. During this time Gabriella was on medication that relaxed her completely. She hardly moved; she seemed to be in a coma.

Father Doug continued to pray and as he did, Gabriella's body began to make a waving movement. It was so strong that Father Doug asked if she was in a coma or not because the movements were so visible. You could tell that the Spirit was working through her. During this prayer time, Gabriella was still undergoing her blood washes. We needed to start with the chemotherapy.

Those who are familiar with this treatment know what a roller coaster ride it can be. The normal protocol for chemotherapy depends on the type you are on. In Gabriella's case, she was on it for five days, then a ten-day wait followed by a bone marrow aspiration to see if the cancer cells had been killed.

The love we were surrounded with was incredible. Phone calls from Italy, calls from our family and friends. It was a blessing in itself to see such love from everyone. Our friends were in the waiting room with homemade goodies, espresso, etc. Each and every one who had any contact with us during this time was a true friend. We cried, we laughed, we prayed and we filled the waiting room with much love, God's love.

The Lord sends us friends and family for a reason. Don't wait for tragedy to hit to let them know how much they mean to you. Let them know today! I think of friends today as God's little elves. He sends them to comfort us, to love us, to share good and bad times. We'll never forget any of our friends and the love they shared with us. May God always bless them.

CHAPTER SEVEN

The Endless Vigil

Come unto Me all of you who are weary and burdened.

~Matthew 11:28

The days and nights seemed endless. A week went by where we'd try to find a couch or chairs to lay our tired bodies. Many times there was nowhere in the hospital for us to sleep, so we didn't sleep at all. Even though Children's Hospital invited us to stay in the Ronald McDonald House, we didn't want to leave the hospital. It got to the point where we'd leave a sweater or jacket on a spot so that when evening came around we'd have somewhere quiet to sleep. But by 7 a.m. we would have to clear out because the offices were open again for the daily appointments.

Even though the days were tough, we managed to

laugh sometimes. I remember a couple of occasions when Johnny had found a gurney in a hallway where he made himself comfortable. He was so tired that he was as still as could be. By morning we had found him, his shoes were under the gurney and he was covered up to his neck, only his head was showing. As we looked above the gurney we saw that the area was a surgical entrance way. We couldn't stop laughing at the sight.

Another time, Gino got that spot first, and he was so tired that he snored all night. At six the next morning the nurses who were beginning their shift kept hearing this roaring sound. It surely wasn't a normal sound, so they followed it to Gino, asleep on the gurney.

I can still see myself sitting outside the ICU, crying, with Gino, Mom, and family, asking why was God punishing us? What was He trying to tell us? Why our daughter? Questions that nobody but He could answer. No matter how much faith I had in God, I knew in my heart that Gabriella wasn't going to be with us for much longer. The big word leukemia would always appear before my eyes. I knew that there were not too many with AMML who are cured. I'd think of how it would be without her. It was an awful thought but could be reality one day. You expect Grandma and Grandpa and Mom and Dad to go home to the Lord first. You don't ever think of your child going before them all. You expect to see your child grow up, go to school, go on dates, get married, and have children of her own. Death never comes to a parent's mind in the early ages.

As the week ended, we were moved to a medical floor where we would spend the next several months. The doctors were amazed that Gabriella made it there at all; they never expected her to come out of the ICU. Again, the grace of God was with us, even though at the time we didn't see it.

Gabriella became more and more like herself, as much as she could under the circumstances. A few days later Father Doug came by again checking on us and a few other families from our parish. We were in Room 52, and the Ross family was in 51. Megan Ross was Gabriella's little next door neighbor. She, like Gabriella, had leukemia. Father Doug suggested that I go and talk to Mrs. Ross, that maybe she could help me get over some of the things I was feeling. She might help me understand what kind of road I had to look forward to.

I went and introduced myself to Mrs. Ross. I shared

with her our situation. One thing I will never forget her saying as she looked into my eyes was, "It is a long, hard road, there is nothing easy about it."

Returning to Gabriella's room, I sat back to think about it all. I knew that no matter what Mrs. Ross told me, I should take it to heart. If Father Doug referred us to the Rosses that was good enough for me; they had to be good people.

As the days went by we really didn't have a whole lot to do with Megan's family. They had their problems, and, boy, did we have ours! To this day I wish I had gotten to know them better during that time. Here were two families from the same church with daughters with the same illness and only six months apart in age. If that wasn't a setup from God, I don't know what is.

Late that afternoon we received the report from the first bone marrow aspiration. We had prayed so hard, but the news wasn't good. The chemotherapy had done nothing. We had been told from the beginning that, due to the type of leukemia Gabriella had, there was only a twenty percent chance of remission, which really isn't much. God's grace would be the only way of healing her. Medicine didn't have good odds. Every time chemotherapy is used, the odds become worse.

As humans we expect our Lord to heal our loved one in times of need. Our faith leads us to believe that miracles will happen, not knowing then what we know now, that our Lord heals in two different ways. There is a physical healing and a spiritual healing. The physical healing is, of course, the illness or problem. The spiritual healing is in growing with our Lord and knowing of all His wonders. If you have to choose between the two, it is better to have a spiritual healing than a physical healing, so you will have eternal life with our Father.

The physical healing is only temporary. Once we die, some sooner, some later, the physical healing won't do you any good. But your spiritual healing will be with you eternally. We always prayed for the wrong healing. Of course, we are only human. Today, I pray for God's will and a spiritual healing for my loved ones.

We have to expect that sometimes our Lord calls our children home early, and we should be grateful knowing that they are at our Lord's side. I truly believe that once our missions are completed here on earth, and our Lord is satisfied with what we have done, He does call us home.

No matter what we do, or what medicine we take, if

His will is for us to go home, that is what will be done. If He is not ready for us, He will heal our illness. Our Lord doesn't want us to suffer. Whenever we are experiencing a tragedy or illness, we need to understand that there is a reason for it all. There is a lesson to be learned. We need to pray and ask our Father to reveal to us what lesson we are to learn from each situation.

Of course, Gino and I are only human, and we always wanted Gabriella to be healed. Oh, how we cried together at times! We wouldn't even have to say anything, just a look, and we could read each other's heart. We tried so hard not to cry in front of Gabriella. But one of us would be holding her and we would look at each other and the tears of fear and sadness would overwhelm us.

It is so important that our loved ones do not see us cry. We are their inspiration. If they see us crying and losing the battle they give up just as fast. Especially with children. They are very sharp. Their moods change as soon as the tone of your voice changes or they see you crying.

I remember waiting for the bone marrow aspiration results to come back. The tension was so heavy, but for Gabriella's sake we would have to play and laugh and continue on with whatever we were doing. Every time the doctor came back with the results—and they weren't ever good—we had to play the pretend game again. At times I would get up and walk away. I'd go into the chapel or outside, just so I could cry and get angry with God again. The only thing that would satisfy me a little was holding her, and squeezing her, and loving her, and absorbing all I could of her while she was still here with us.

We learned to treasure everything she did, everything she said, and we locked it up in the deepest part of our hearts. Those are the best kinds of pictures to treasure.

There were so many times we just wanted to give up. Only by keeping our faith in God and knowing His will is to be done could we go on, one day at a time.

We continued to thank God that Gabriella wasn't sick from the chemotherapy. She continued to sing and dance. Her appetite was still good, she was alert, she was not bedridden. We keep thanking God for that wonderful gift, not having to see our Little Angel suffer. As parents, you know that when our children are hurt or sick we would give anything for it to be us and not them.

CHAPTER EIGHT

What True Love Is

Never be lacking in zeal, but keep your spiritual fervor, serving the Lord. Be joyful in hope, patient in affliction, faithful in prayer. Share with God's people who are in need. Practice hospitality.

~Romans 12:11-13

I t was family meeting time now. We met in the conference room with our doctor and he was very straightforward about the whole situation. It wasn't any surprise to us that things were not looking good. He said they had a few more types of chemotherapy treatments they could try, but they hadn't had much success with them. We were willing to try anything.

Gabriella was to be given a Hickman catheter, which is a tube that is surgically inserted into the chest area and sticks out through the skin so that all medicine and intravenous treatment could be given through it. The treatment was preferable to starting an IV with a needle again and again. It is usually done with a patient who will have long-term treatments and medicine. Even though it was another surgery for Gabriella and another traumatic moment for us, it really is better for the patient. So off she went again into surgery, and before we knew it, it was over and done with.

July 2 came so fast. It was Gabriella's second birthday. We had asked if she could go onto the private patio area outside her room. We were told she could as long as she wore a face mask. It was very important that she not be exposed to germs because the chemotherapy was destroying her resistance and any infection could kill her. Family members and a few close and dear friends were there as we prepared for the party. It seems pretty weird that everybody had thought of bringing their camera but when the time came, nobody had one.

All along, Gabriella had not been allowed to hold or even to be with her baby brother Gianluca. She would only see him through the window of her room. We were around her with all kinds of gifts, but she was only interested in one gift—to hold her baby brother in her arms. She kept reaching for him. Finally we let her sit down on a blanket that was spread out on the cement and handed the baby to her. She finally got to hold him and oh, what tenderness she had for him! He was almost bigger than she was, but she managed. She looked at him and caressed his face as though she was the mom. Her gentle, fragile hand was so precious; she kissed him and loved him the whole time.

Gabriella didn't want the other gifts she had there; the best gift ever was her baby. It made many of us come to realize that material gifts are only temporary things, but true, unconditional love is everlasting. We wished we'd had a camera to capture this picture of true love, but what better picture than the one she carved into our hearts at that moment? We didn't need any picture to remind us, our hearts and minds would keep that vision of love safe and near us always.

By now everybody there was as quiet as could be, absorbing the moment of shared love. Tears were flowing all around us. What a gift—God's true love.

Sometimes in life we tend to forget what true love is. We need to take a moment each day to hug and to love those who are near and dear to us, because the time will come when the only things we have left are the memories of the moments.

We had a lovely birthday party. There were sad moments and happy ones, all very special. As the hours went by, Gabriella's time to get back into her room drew near. Oh, the tears! She was so heartbroken, I would have given anything to have stopped the pain and sadness that filled her. It took quite a while to calm her down that afternoon.

Time seemed to fly by. It was July 10, the day scheduled for Luigi's gallbladder surgery. Gino and I took Luigi to Children's Hospital in Los Angeles. Gianluca was with my Aunt Carmela. Mom and Dad stayed with Gabriella who was undergoing a course of chemotherapy at the time. We wanted to be with her but we had to take care of Luigi, too.

The surgery was supposed to last a couple of hours. After four hours had gone by, my heart was telling me something wasn't right. As we began to get restless, Dr. Hansen walked into the room. He explained to us that there were complications and they had to re-evaluate the situation. The surgery was not successful because of Luigi's birth problem in the stomach area. The liver is attached to the top of the gallbladder, and when they tried to remove the gallbladder they began having problems. They tried to just flush the stone out instead, but they couldn't find it, not even with the x-ray at time of surgery, so they chose to close him up and hope all would go well.

Evening was here, and Gino and I were upset that Luigi had to go through all of this only to find that nothing could be done. I understand sometimes these things happen, and we didn't blame anyone, I was just mad. We had been there since 6 a.m. I sent Gino home around 11 that night. A friend of ours offered to drive him to San Diego, more than two-and-a-half hours away, so he could be with Gabriella.

Luigi was sitting up by evening of the first day, and soon he was walking the halls of the hospital, with staples all the way down his stomach. God has always given Luigi an especially fast recovery time that amazes his doctors.

I was torn between two hospitals with one child in each. Even though he was older, Luigi was still a mama's boy and wanted me there. On the other hand, I had my baby undergoing chemotherapy, not knowing when the Lord would call her home. I missed her smile. I missed her! Sometimes life isn't fair, but we have to get our strength from God. We must ask Him to build our faith and help us get through each day that comes our way.

Only the Lord can help us through something like this.

I pray for those who are going through rough times in their lives. I ask the Lord to touch those who are lost. To help them find their way to Him. He is our only salvation.

So many times in our lives we don't understand why certain things happen to us, why there is such suffering, why so much illness. When the hard times come our way it is very easy to get mad, angry, violent, lonely, mean, and sometimes suicidal. We even think of turning away from our Lord. But that is when we need to remember that the Lord our God is our Father, and he doesn't want harm to come to His children. God has His plan for us so we can't change anything. We can only deal with our challenges and learn from them, for the Lord is with us always.

Sickness and troubles don't come from the Lord. But I believe that our Lord sits back and watches to see if we go His way. I'm sure it makes Him very happy when we turn the situation over to Him and truly give it up. And when we're still able to smile, pray, and most of all, give thanks, well, that's true love and true faith. Faith in His will, not ours.

It's so easy to say, "Oh yes, Lord, whatever is Your

will." But really, how easy is it to truly believe in it? To have faith in the Lord's will is a gift. A gift that I have been blessed with. It's so much easier to see things through God's eyes rather than our eyes. We will always see things as much worse than He does. And yes, death and illnesses are very serious matters, but since we have no choice in life we have to deal with our situations. God is there waiting to walk us through our deepest valleys. And when we walk with Him, what love, what warmth, what peace we find.

Luigi was discharged from the hospital and then spent a week in Palm Springs at my parents' house, so that I could be with Gabriella. The whole time Luigi was recovering, Gabriella asked for him. We had to explain to her that Luigi had "owies" and he couldn't be with us now.

Finally the day arrived when Luigi came to visit his sister. He had been missing her terribly. When she saw him, she wrinkled up her nose and smiled from ear to ear. She held him and loved him. How she loved her brothers!

We were into another month, undergoing another course of chemotherapy, and still no remission. Things were looking worse. Again, the waiting game—five days of chemotherapy, wait ten days, and then the bone mar-

row aspiration. Only to find out it didn't take again. The
roller coaster ride you're on under a chemotherapy treatment procedure is very emotional. You need to keep a
grip on reality. Your mind can play so many games with
you.

It was now around the end of July. We began going
home to sleep. It was a little easier leaving Gabriella
alone. We'd leave while she was sleeping so it wouldn't
hurt her as much. We couldn't stay another night; we
were becoming useless to her during the day because we
were so tired.

During that time my cousin had brought over a "Little
Mermaid" videotape. Gabriella had never been much for
TV, but she began watching the Little Mermaid over and
over again. It was as if she felt the freedom of the mermaid. She sang along with all the songs. She'd be having
her chemotherapy treatment and still she'd be singing and
dancing to the tape. The nurses would have to keep coming in and straightening out her IV lines; they would curl
up to nothing several times a day.

The whole time Gabriella was undergoing chemotherapy she had hardly any side effects. One day Gino asked
the doctor if it was normal for a child to undergo so many

treatments and still be running, jumping, and singing; it was as if she were drinking a glass of milk rather than the medication. She was truly blessed by God because she should have been very sick from the treatments and the types of chemotherapy she was on. Yet, they weren't making her feel bad. Unfortunately, they weren't killing the cancer cells either.

The hospital staff was very thoughtful. They had offered us a room at the Ronald McDonald house. We never did use it; we wanted to be at Gabriella's side as much as possible, and when it was time to go home, we had two boys waiting for a little of Mom and Dad's love. So we returned the keys and gave the room up to another family.

Whoever would have thought we would be on the list for a room at the Ronald McDonald house again one day.

CHAPTER NINE

Home from the Hospital

Because you have seen Me, you have believed.
Blessed are those who have not seen and yet
have believed.

~John 20:29

L uigi spent most of his days with me, while Gianluca spent most of his at my aunt's and uncle's house. They had raised him from two months old. As the months passed by, Gianluca was growing without us around him, but I knew he was in good hands. Now August 17 was here. Luigi was going to be 13 years old. It was a special birthday for him, too, after his surgery and all. Our dear friends Bill and Mary Mayo stayed with Gabriella while we had a gathering with family for Luigi's birthday.

It was so hard to enjoy the gathering knowing that Gabriella was in the hospital so sick, but we managed to pull it off for Luigi. Our hearts weren't there, but we knew we had to get over our feelings and do our best. It seemed our life was only her and the hospital. Just holding her, seeing her smile, hearing her sing to the mermaid, would ease any pain that was in our hearts.

The days were so long. They seemed as though they would never be over. But then, looking back, how fast the time flew! It was a blessing that I wasn't working so I was able to stay with Gabriella each and every day. And Gino's office was only a few exits away on the freeway. He was able to see his customers and to do some of his work from Gabriella's room. We thank God for the love and kindness all his coworkers had for us during those days. They all showed true friendship and love.

Days passed and Gabriella wasn't showing any signs of remission. We knew in our hearts that the farther we got into the chemotherapy treatments the less chance we had to get her into remission, even though she didn't seem to be suffering from any side effects, which was great.

As the treatments continued, we continued to pray that our Heavenly Father would give us the miracle that Gabriella would go into remission. One day I walked into her room after she and Gino had had a deep conversation. Gino had an overwhelmed look on his face. As I came in I asked what was going on.

He began to explain to me what had happened, then he turned to Gabriella.

"Gabriella *a papa*," he asked, "did you say *Buon giorno* (meaning good morning) to Jesus?"

"Yes," she said but the serious look on her face indicated that it went way beyond that.

Gino asked her, "Gabriella, where's Jesus?"

She answered very slowly, raising her eyes, and with her little finger pointing up she said, "Up and down, up and down."

There was no joke about it, she was as serious as could be. And she was only two years old, there was no way she could have made it up.

"Did Jesus talk to you, Gabriella?" Gino continued.

"No," she replied, "*uno bacetto*," meaning a kiss.

Not only did our Lord come down to visit her, He gave her a kiss on her cheek. It seemed that He had visited her on more than one occasion. It appeared that it had happened before because she spoke about his going up and down, up and down; meaning that He came down, went up, and did it again.

We always knew there was something special about

our daughter. This just proved to us once again that she was chosen by our Lord. No matter what would happen, we knew He was with her always.

We often noticed hospital employees looking through the window of Gabriella's room. I'd ask if I could help them and there was always the same response; they had heard about the little two-year-old angel who was undergoing chemotherapy and dancing at the same time. It was just too strange for a cancer patient receiving chemotherapy to be so active. Again, that showed us how special she was. Then reality would set in. We knew she wasn't getting better and we had no control over the cancer. It was winning. But in the long run, Gabriella was still winning the real fight. She was on her way home to our Father in heaven to have eternal life with him.

Days were flying by. When evening would set in and it would be time to leave Gabriella for the night, it was very difficult. But I did have a baby at home, and Luigi, who had just had surgery. They needed us just as much as Gabriella did. I'm sure they felt abandoned. We tried to juggle the best we possibly could.

One day while I was at the hospital I heard that a newborn diagnosed with AMML was transferred in. I could only think of what the parents might be feeling at that moment, remembering what we had felt. I sensed their pain. I knocked on the door to their room and introduced myself. I told them a little about us and we spoke for awhile. I remember sharing a few novenas and scriptures that had comforted me. I just wanted them to know they weren't alone, that someone was there if they needed to talk or just a shoulder to cry on.

About three weeks later I asked about them and was told that the baby girl had responded very well to treatment and was sent home, and that she would continue treatments as an outpatient. Sometimes we as humans need to see a physical healing also. I never did find out how she was doing after she left. May God's blessing be upon her and keep her safe.

I must confess that when I found out the baby had gone into remission I congratulated her parents and wished them the best, but then I left the room crying and wondering selfishly, why her and not Gabriella? I ran sobbing to the chapel.

"Why, God, why not my Gabriella? Why the baby? Is she more special than my little girl?"

I hurt so bad in the deepest part of my heart. I felt that

I must not be good enough, nor was my daughter. I later realized what I was doing and asked my Lord to forgive the feelings I had, the selfishness I felt, the loneliness that surrounded me.

Time continued to pass. New children were admitted with cancer or leukemia, new ones would come and others would go. Some would go home to our Lord. And, oh, those children! You could see them in the doctors' and nurses' faces. Sadness was all around us. All the prayers, all the medical assistance, but nothing can stop God's will.

By now we were into October. Gabriella was going to have her sixth treatment. We prayed about it and had decided to go ahead with it. We had been told this particular treatment could kill her, that her heart probably couldn't handle the strength of the medicine, nor could the rest of her organs. We had been told that it could cause brain damage, kidney failure, lung collapse, or turn her into a vegetable.

By the time we finished the five-day course, she had changed completely. This time we could tell it was too much for her little body. Just looking at her we could see that she had had enough. We still managed to get a little smile here and there, but this one slowed her down.

Her most joyful times now were spent with her brothers. How she waited for the days when she could see those brothers! She loved Luigi so much. He spent every day by her side, and when we brought Gianluca in she would feed him and love him. She wanted him in bed with her. We took pictures of her lying in her bed with her baby by her side taking a nap. What precious times those were! We began to bring Gianluca in more often because it was the only thing that would bring joy to her face.

Ten days had gone by after the chemotherapy, and the bone marrow was clean. We were so happy! Then we waited five more days to redo the aspiration. The doctor told us that a bone biopsy had been taken at the same time because it goes even deeper than the aspiration. We were so afraid to let ourselves get excited, but fifteen days went by and still she was clean. Three more weeks, and still nothing.

Another biopsy was taken because the blood tests were showing that the cells weren't reproducing due to the strength of the chemotherapy. It had killed off all the cells, and the body was not producing anything, neither good cells nor bad cells. It was time for Gino and me to decide: if the cancer did come back, what was our next step?

Dr. Kadota came in with the biopsy test results and there was one cell in there. And, of course, one cell is too many. So we talked about the last treatment that was available to her and decided to go for it.

Five more days of chemotherapy. During this time, Gabriella began to go into a deep depression. She wouldn't talk anymore; she only moaned. She didn't want the TV on, nor did she want the window blinds open. She ate nothing and drank nothing. She had sores all over her mouth and down her throat. She had a rash on her bottom that was so raw it bled all the time. Diarrhea caused by the chemotherapy would flush out of her; we could hardly clean her and couldn't even put a diaper on her.

It was surely a mistake to have put her through the last treatment, and for what? It didn't work anyway. Oh, how miserable she was. It was so hard as parents to see our child in so much pain and not be able to do anything about it. I would have cut off my arm if it would have lessened her suffering.

She slept for hours and hours in our arms; she didn't want us to leave her alone. She slept moaning and groaning. She didn't care who was there. We then decided—no more chemo, no more medicine, no more pain for our child. If God was going to heal her, this was the time, if it was His will.

Dr. Kadota came in and told us what our alternatives were. If we wanted to, we could take her home, or let her pass on in the hospital and they would make her as comfortable as possible. Or they could give her treatments that could help their experiments towards knowledge about different medicines. He said we could take a few days to decide what we wanted to do. He left the room, and Gino and I looked at each other. We knew what we wanted. We wanted her home with us, no matter how long it was going to be.

So Gino ran after the doctor and walked him back into the room. We told him we wanted to take her home. He asked us several times if we wanted to think about it, that he'd give us the weekend to think it over. We explained to him that it was time to bring Gabriella home, that her life has been in God's hands and her death would be also, that whatever time the Lord was going to give us, we wanted her to enjoy it at home. No doctors, no medicine, no pain.

Then I had to go downstairs for coffee, with a visit to

the chapel to lift my daughter to our Lord to do His will.

As I was returning to Gabriella's room, I heard laughing, and the mermaid cartoon was playing once again. When I walked into the room, much to my surprise she was smiling and singing once again. Talk about prayers being answered Federal Express! I asked Gino what had happened to turn her spirits so completely around.

He said, "I told Gabriella she was going home."

I took one look at her and she looked like the Gabriella I once knew.

We wanted to take her home that evening, but of course that wasn't possible. We had to prepare many things before leaving the hospital. That evening, Kathy, in the Child Life Program, asked the doctor if Gabriella could go into the playroom. She had taken the time to clean the toys so that Gabriella wouldn't catch anything. The doctor said that would be a great idea. Then he turned to us.

"You've made the right decision. Quality of time versus quantity of time," he said and smiled.

So off we went walking down the hallway with Gabriella. Her eyes had gotten so large; she couldn't believe she was leaving her room. As we approached the playroom she stood there for a while not knowing what to do. In the playroom the family sat around her—Dad, Grandma, Grandpa, her brothers, cousins, aunts and myself. We were the only ones there along with Kathy. Gabriella began to loosen up a little. She began to paint, play, laugh, and just have fun. Just like a two-year-old should be. When it was time to leave, she cried. She didn't want to go. We had to walk her around for a while; there was no way she was going back to her room. She only knew she was going home and she wanted it to be now. We had been out of her room for several hours and had to get back, but she continued to cry. It took a long time to get her to sleep that night. Was it a mistake letting her know she was going home?

Thursday arrived, and she could say only one thing—*home.* All day long she kept waiting to go home. It was a difficult day. Nothing we said made her happy. By evening, again, she did not want to stay in her room. She only wanted to go home; and she was angry with us. She probably thought we were teasing her. How could we make her understand that Friday was the big day?

At last Friday was here and we packed up all her gifts and belongings. They filled two minivans!

When it was finally time to go home she didn't believe us anymore; we had cried wolf too many times. As we got into the van, she became quieter than ever. The whole ride, she'd only stare out the window. She didn't believe she was really going home until we drove up our driveway. When our little dog jumped all over her she finally smiled. We carried her into the house and her smile was from ear to ear. Joy filled her heart! We went right to her toy room which was located underneath the staircase in the downstairs hallway. Then she sat down on the floor and played with her brothers and her cousin Sabrina and the dog. She was so happy, so joyful, so loved by all around her.

Later that afternoon the nurse from Hospice Care came by. She needed to teach me how to take care of Gabriella's IV and the antibiotic that she would need. During this time I had to continuously remind Gabriella that Mom and Dad were going to take care of her now. No more doctors, no more hospitals. She was so content with everything around her.

By morning she was doing quite well. Not really knowing what to expect and remembering the doctor's words—seven to ten days was all we'd have with her—

we thanked God for every morning that we saw her smiling face. When we were in the kitchen and Gino asked her if she wanted breakfast, she replied in her sweet voice.

"Yes! No pancake, no eggs."

Gabriella was so sick of always having the same thing to eat.

That day we went for a walk. She loved to walk with me, so we went down about two blocks to the pool. As she looked through the gates I could read her thoughts. She was remembering all the fun she had had there. Then slowly she pulled herself away and began to walk back home. There was no way that I was going to be allowed to help her. She could do it herself. As fragile as she was, she still continued to show me the inner strength that she had. The kind of strength that only our Lord fills you with.

Each night for the first week, Hospice Care came over to check Gabriella's blood levels on an ongoing basis, to keep up with what was going on in her little body. She did extremely well at home. She ate well and she played. She didn't miss anything. If it wasn't made obvious by her hair loss, you'd never know that she was so sick.

On her first Sunday home, which was October 18, we

took her to our 6 p.m. church service, where all our friends in Christ gathered together in singing and praising our Lord. When the services were to begin, Father Doug Regan asked us to bring Gabriella up to the altar. As we approached the altar, he asked everybody to raise their hands and pray for Gabriella. He briefly explained to the parishioners that she was one of the children we had been praying so hard for, for God's healing. He went on to say that she was sent home to pass on to eternal life with our Lord in heaven.

Gino was holding her at this time. Father's hands were laid on her along with Gino's and mine. As we looked into the gathering there were tears upon so many faces. And love on each and every one. The Holy Spirit had filled the whole gathering. We could feel the presence of the Lord and all His mighty angels.

I recalled an experience I had had when I was young, a vision that has come to me many times since then. It started when I was a child living in a large custom-built home in Hawthorne, California. During the darkest hours of the night I'd be sleeping, and yet I could see myself looking out the window of my bedroom (which was up-stairs). As I gazed out of my window I would see an awesome scene in the heavens. The sky would be filled with pastel colors and people would be moving about. There was a man sitting on a throne in the center of it all. He was a bearded man, older, with long white hair. He would be watching all that was going on around him and gazing into the faces of the men and women. They appeared to be people from the past. People I'd read about in school. St. Joseph, angels, prophets, other saints. It seemed as though it was a peek into heaven! It was like watching a drive-in movie outside my window!

This vision happened quite often. I still don't know if it was my soul that was looking out the window while my body was sleeping. I only know that it seemed so real. Even today I continue to have this "peek into heaven."

CHAPTER TEN

Truly an Angel

Behold, I send an angel before you to keep you in the way and to bring you into the place which I have prepared.

~Exodus 23:20

Nearly three weeks had passed. Gabriella was still with us but we could tell she was deteriorating. She did everything a little more slowly. Her blood transfusions weren't really helping her anymore. We tried to keep our faith up through those dark days. We hoped and prayed that the Lord would grant us the physical healing. But the leukemia was taking over her whole body. We got to the point where we didn't want to know any of the CBC (complete blood count) levels; it wasn't important to us anymore. All that mattered was enjoying every minute of each day with her and cherishing all the memories.

Not only did we cherish each moment we had together, Gabriella did, too. Every time she looked at us, she'd look into the deepest part of our soul. She, too, was storing it all. Each hug wasn't just a hug, each one had something special behind it. She was preparing her memories, just as we were.

Then for some strange reason Gabriella's hemoglobin blood count went up. The nurse had taken it on the morning of the 6th of November and, much to her surprise, the counts were looking very good. She had the tests repeated once more and they didn't change. Gabriella was looking rather well. We were all quite shocked.

On November 7, the whole family took Gabriella to Disneyland. She was still managing to have good days; she still sang and danced. We didn't realize how sick she looked until we got the pictures back from the developers and saw how pale and fragile she appeared. Gino and I took her for a hot dog near the Dumbo ride. The music was playing and we videotaped her dancing and eating at the same time. She was so full of joy always. So happy, not even death would take away the gift of joy that our Father in heaven had given her. We know in our hearts that our Lord lent us His hand in the results of the tests so that we would have enough confidence to take her on this trip. There was no other explanation as to why her tests were the way they were.

As the days went by, Gabriella continued to hold her own. She loved to feed her brother Gianluca, who was seven months old by now. She loved Luigi more than words could say. She was so full of love; only someone touched by an angel could love so much. She would hold her baby so tenderly that our hearts would melt. Her love penetrated everyone she touched. It's hard to describe the unconditional love she had. To her it came so naturally. For us, well, sometimes we have to work at it.

On November 10 from 12 midnight on the alarm on Gabriella's IV kept going off. I did everything possible to get it to work, but there was no way to stop the alarm. Nothing was working, even though I had called Hospice Care to walk me through the steps and I was doing everything right. Then, out of nowhere, it stopped ringing. At 3:15 a.m. I went back to bed.

Now wide awake, I lay in bed praying. As I was lying there, a bright light lit up the room. There were two heavenly angels. They were at least six and a half feet tall and strong looking. I knew they were male angels because of their size. Their hands were crossed before them as they looked down upon me. I couldn't see their faces but I could see the whole being, their flowing gowns and long, silky hair. They were so gentle and peaceful. I tried to move my right hand to wake up Gino, but my arm wouldn't move. I had no feeling in it. The more I tried to move it, the less I could feel.

The angels' wings weren't opened; they were at their sides. They never said anything to me but made me understand that this was not for Gino but only for me. They never spoke, yet I heard them say this to my heart. They sent a sense of peace and serenity throughout the room. The love and warmth was everywhere. A few minutes went by, or maybe it was only moments, but it seemed like a long time. I finally got to sleep.

In the morning I shared the experience with my family. I described the light, the glow, the silhouettes, and then the angels appearing. I told them about the incredible experience I had with the angels. In my heart I believed that Gabriella would be healed because I'd had a visit from two angels.

As I was telling them about the experience, I wondered if they would believe that I had truly had an encounter with angels. I remember promising God that no matter what, I was going to share this wonderful gift, whether or not I was believed. I knew that the Lord would touch those who needed to be touched. My job from this point on was to share what had happened to me on November 10, 1992.

Saturday, Gabriella was excited that her cousin Sabrina was coming over. She loved her so much. They were true buddies. Gabriella was surrounded by all who loved her. She managed to play a little and rest a little. Then, around four in the afternoon, she insisted she had to go shopping. We wondered where this was coming from. She kept saying, "Mama's birthday, and we need to go shopping!" And she wouldn't give up until we said yes.

When we got to the Carlsbad mall she wanted French fries and then to go to the birthday store and Bullock's "Christmas store." Those were her choices. While I was buying the French fries, she saw across the way the small store that sold all types of birthday items. She made my mom carry her in there to buy some birthday stickers.

Then Gabriella wanted to go into the Christmas store. She pointed out where she wanted to be and then guided her grandmother to the angel tree. She picked out six angels from the tree and handed them to her, then picked some out for her Nonna, her other grandma, too. At the time we thought, how sweet! Never expecting what was to come. Our Lord prepared her so she could prepare us. But we weren't catching on.

Two hours had passed, and we thought it was time to take her home. We had done only the things she wanted to do, and that was enough.

While were on our way home, my sister brought it to my attention that Gabriella's breathing pattern had changed radically. So I attended to her, thinking probably the outing was too much for her. As the evening progressed she began to get worse. We called the hospice nurse to observe her and tell us what was going on.

Of course she said she was getting worse, something we didn't want to hear. We put her on some oxygen, which seemed to calm her down a little. During the night she used the oxygen off and on.

Sunday was my birthday. The whole family stayed close together and shared as much as we could. My dad cooked a lovely dinner and we all sat down at the table around three in the afternoon. Gabriella wasn't doing very well. After asking her several times to come to the table and eat a little, she had me carry her to it. We sat there and she rested her head on my shoulder for a while. Then she sat up and took three bites of pasta, and that was the last time she ate. She gave me the honor of sitting at the table for my birthday dinner, she ate a little, and that was it. It was enough to exhaust her completely.

We still managed to get Gabriella to our 6 p.m. service. It was important to us to have her there. We knew in our hearts she would be leaving us soon, but our faith kept us going. We wanted her to be completely filled with love. I'm sure it was for us, too; it would help us feel better.

During the service Gabriella slept most of the time. Afterward there was a healing service. We took her up to Deacon Bob for hands-on healing and prayer.

Our friends and loved ones surrounded us with love, prayers and strength. I was so grateful for all the special people our Lord has sent into our lives. We couldn't go through this without them.

When the prayer time was over, Deacon Bob left the altar area and went into the back room. Later we found out that he had been spiritually wiped out during Gabriella's prayer time. But during his brief retreat, he must have gotten a message from God because as he approached us again, he told us that Gabriella was to receive the body of Christ. He went up to her and asked her if she knew who the Lord Jesus Christ was and would she accept him.

"Yes," Gabriella replied. Then she bowed her head and received her first Holy Communion.

It was a very honorable moment and very important to us, as Catholics. And I thought my birthday dinner was special! Who'd ever think that my daughter would receive her first Holy Communion that evening? This was a very special event because children don't receive their communion until the age of seven or more. We'll be forever thankful to Deacon Bob for listening to our Lord. As we were leaving, much to our surprise a dear lady from our church ran up behind us and said, "Gabriella's certificate of Holy Communion will be in the mail tomorrow morning!" She had caught us off guard because our understanding was that nobody knew what was going on. Later we found out she had also received word from the Lord to do so.

Sunday night Gabriella required more oxygen than during the day. We carried her upstairs to bed, where she slept peacefully all night long. I slept with her that night.

As I'd lie by her side I'd hug her and love her, trying to capture as much as I could. I'd lie down on the floor some also, but I didn't want to leave her side. I knew in my heart she wasn't going to be with us much longer.

I'd never prayed as hard as I did that evening. Actually, in the previous five months it seemed as though that's all I found myself doing. I'd wake up thanking God for the new morning, pray during the day while we had our ups and downs, and as evening approached I'd thank Him for all the blessings He had given us during the day and pray for Him to watch over us during the night. Next morning I'd wake up and do it all over again.

Monday morning we asked the hospice nurse to come. She checked Gabriella out and told us that her time was close. But, of course, we didn't want to accept that. How could she die when I had had a visit from two angels? Didn't that mean anything? Wasn't that a sign that she was going to be healed? Does that happen with everyone who is going to die?

I was so confused, I couldn't understand anything now. Where was my God when I needed Him so much? Why wasn't He making her better rather than worse? Why wasn't He listening to my prayers?

My head felt like a tether ball, bouncing all around, never stopping for a moment. When thoughts of death would come I'd freeze up. How could I live without my little girl, our princess? What about all those dreams and plans we had for her? They didn't mean a thing. Obviously God had different plans for her. Something more everlasting than anything she could have here on earth.

Monday wasn't a good day. She hadn't eaten anything, nor did she drink anything. We tried everything—chicken soup, fresh farm eggs, anything we could think of. I even tried to feed her soup by syringe; I cut off the tip of it to make the hole bigger so the soup could pass through. I thought if I kept her eating and drinking she would keep her strength. I didn't realize that some of her body organs were already shutting down, so the body no longer required food or water.

Monday night I hooked up her IV thinking some fluids would be good for her during the night. Gino carried the IV pole up and I carried her. As I did, I felt in my heart that this was the last time I would ever carry her upstairs; it was a dreadful feeling. I kept those thoughts and feelings to myself, but I did tell Gino just before entering Gabriella's bedroom that I thought it would be better if she slept with us. I just didn't like the way she was breathing.

All night we were awake; Gabriella was very restless. Around two in the morning, she began to experience pain in her head. We decided to disconnect her from the IV. It was obvious our daughter was going to go home to our Lord soon. By this time we had given her Tylenol with codeine, hoping the pain would go away. Gino didn't want her on morphine. His father had required morphine just before dying, and I think that giving Gabriella morphine would have made it more final to him. It would mean that she was on her deathbed. So I honored his request.

The Tylenol did nothing. I could only pray that God would stop the pain. "Take her, oh Lord, but don't let her suffer," that's all I could think of.

Mom, Gino and I were on the bed with Gabriella. I could only listen to her moan, I couldn't take the pain away. She'd hold her head and look at me.

Finally I said, "Gabriella *a mama*, you have big *booas* (pain), huh?"

"Yes," she said.

"Gabriella," I continued, "if you close your eyes and

go to Jesus, all your *booas* will be gone. Go. Go."

She turned slowly toward me. I kissed her. She stared into my eyes and gasped for air, continuing to stare at me. Her body and soul were fighting, and then she was gone. My baby was gone, now free from all pain. She had waited for me to release her from this world. She wanted me to tell her it was okay to go, she had my permission.

I want to share with those experiencing a situation with someone they love who is dying. It's so important that we let our loved ones go. We mustn't try to hold them against their will. They need to be free, free of this world of pain, free to go home to our Lord. No matter what their age is, they still want us to tell them it's okay to die.

We all seemed to handle it pretty well although I believe that we are never really ready for death. I believe we gain a better understanding of it, but once a loved one is gone the pain transfers over to us. But our Lord is good. He gives us the strength to get through our deepest valleys no matter what the situation is, even when death knocks at our door.

I held Gabriella in my arms and kissed her for the last time. How could she be gone? She felt so warm, so good, she seemed as though she were sleeping. I passed her into her father's arms and he caressed her and loved her until it was time to call the hospice nurse and Father T.J. from our church.

My aunt and uncle arrived. They loved her so much! My Uncle Carlo couldn't handle seeing her, but Aunt Carmela came up to our room. She knelt down and wept.

"Gabriella, Gabriella, *bella* Gabriella!" she cried.

I needed to go and wake up Luigi. I wasn't sure how to go about this. I didn't want to scare him but I did want him to see her before she was taken away. I prayed all the way down the hallway for the Lord to make this easier.

I called his name gently, and as he woke up I said, "Luigi, it's time to say good-bye to your sister." He looked at me as though I were speaking another language. I helped him down the hall; he was still half asleep as he entered my room.

When I told him that Gabriella had died and she was on her way to see Jesus in heaven, he began to cry. His heart was broken in half. He felt that part of him had died with his sister. I asked him if he wanted to hold her and I could tell he was afraid. I told him that it was his choice. Finally he did. I sat down at his side while he held her.

Continuing to cry, he said, "I had so many plans for

us, so many things to do, and now, nothing." He was crying like a baby, his tears falling on his sister's face. There
was so much love between brother and sister; unconditional, true, warm love.

Once again I took Gabriella into my arms. It was as
though I couldn't get enough of her. Father T.J. and the
hospice nurse arrived at the same time.

Father embraced us and had comforting words for us.
He then blessed and anointed Gabriella. She had touched
his life in such a special way. Through her, his life had
changed. I guess we can say that all those who encoun-
tered Gabriella were touched by an angel, for she was
truly an angel.

CHAPTER ELEVEN

God will Provide

The Lord is my shepherd; I shall not want.
~Psalm 23:1

We had made arrangements for Eternal Hills Mortuary to pick Gabriella up at 5 a.m. It had to be the hardest thing ever that we had to do. Gino insisted on carrying his daughter in his arms down the stairs. His tears were rapidly falling onto her face as he stared at her, not really believing what was happening. Sadness filled every room of our home. The quietness was overwhelming.

I was still wondering, why had those angels appeared and yet Gabriella was gone? With a better understanding and a closer walk with our Lord, we have realized why the angels came. The angels had appeared in my room at 3:15 a.m. Tuesday morning one week before Gabriella passed away. The same time, same day, and same place one week later. Was it only a coincidence? We now believe they were messengers of God sent to prepare us and to give us peace and serenity so that we could continue on with His plan for our lives. It was so that we could be evangelists of Our Lord, to bring people to better understand certain situations and help those whose lives are filled with misery and pain. Life goes on. We have to continue and we have to bring as many as we can to know who Jesus Christ is, so that they can become part of His kingdom in heaven.

Until this day, I don't know who the two angels were nor do I know their names. Maybe one day soon the Lord will reveal that to me, but for now I can only thank Him and praise Him for the beautiful gifts He has given me, the gifts of peace in my heart, serenity in all I do, and the wonderful gift of faith. Faith that all that He does is good. For He is a God of love and kindness. He is a merciful God. And through Him all good things come.

As we left the house, we found the van from the mortuary waiting for us. We both kissed our daughter for the last time as Gino laid her on the stretcher. He looked at the attendant and said, "Please take care of my angel." He handed the attendant her "binky." He placed it by her side, and the doors closed. Everyone returned to the house except for Gino and me. We stood in the driveway waiting for the van to drive back by as it made its way around our block. When it came by, it slowed down for the speed bump, and as it was passing, we saw a shooting star above it! It shot completely across the sky as though Gabriella were telling us, "Mom, Dad, I'm okay! I'm going home now!" And then it was gone. As the star disappeared from sight, so was the van with our daughter's shell. Her soul was on its way to heaven.

Gino and I stood outside holding and comforting each other. Not one word was said; we knew what the other was feeling, for we both had lost something so dear to us. She was ours. Everyone feels pain when they lose someone they love but, unless they have experienced it, they can't comprehend the anguish in the heart of a parent who loses a child.

We made our way back into the house, where our family members had gathered. We looked like we had gone through a tornado; we were all a wreck. I wanted only to lie down so that I could sleep—to sleep so that I wouldn't have to deal with the reality that she was gone; so that I could dream of her and be with her again. Anything but face the fact that I would never see her again.

Why? Why did this happen? Why didn't my God help her? Why did she have to die? What did we do wrong in life to be tortured like this? So many questions ran through my head, so many whys with no real answers. We missed the physical part of her. We missed her smile. How are we going to live without her? How can life go on without her? I prayed, Oh, Lord, take away the pain, the emptiness, the hollowness I feel in my whole body. Will I ever get better? I just want to scream to the top of the heavens, Oh, Lord, where are You! Why? Why?

We were so exhausted. Only a few hours had passed and it seemed as though a year had gone by. What was it going to be like when time does go by. I needed to come to the reality that all the doctors were gone—hospitals, medications, pain, and my Gabriella was gone along with them all.

Word had gotten around quickly. The phone was ringing off the hook. So many friends and relatives. So much love everybody was showing. Food was coming from all directions. The compassion everybody showed was unbelievable. What dear friends the Lord had blessed us with.

At three in the afternoon we were supposed to go down to the mortuary. Just the thought of it made me ill. I knew it had to be done; there was no way to get around it. Mom, my cousin Johnny, Gino and I went to make the arrangements. As we sat there, not one word was said by any of us. I was just thinking that my baby was here. Was she cold, was she lonely? What silly things come to our mind when we are overwhelmed with grief. I couldn't think straight. I knew it was only her shell, but it was hard to think that way all the time. You know, we are human, so I guess it's okay to think that way sometimes.

Our name was called and we were taken into another room by a gentleman. He told us most of the arrangements had been made; all we had to do was pick out a casket. We walked into a large, cold room. There were four or five styles. I was anxious to get out of there and I knew which one I wanted; I didn't want to hear of anything else. We picked a small white one with angels around it. It was just right for an angel. We had to leave quickly. It was so difficult; there was no way we could stay any longer.

We then had to go down to the burial grounds to find the plot we wanted. We were told about the children's section called "Court of Consecration" and went down to look at the three plots that were available. We chose the one closest to the walkway, and that was enough of that, too. We couldn't handle that very well either; it was just too soon. My daughter was alive thirteen hours ago and now we're here. But we knew it needed to be done, so we went back to the mortuary office to take care of some final details.

We asked the attendant where our friend's daughter was buried. He put her name into the computer and said, "Are you ready? Your daughter will be holding hands side by side with your friend's little girl!" How amazing that was. Neither Gino nor I had been able to attend Megan's burial because Gabriella was having a blood transfusion that day and we needed to be with her. When we heard where Megan was buried, we knew it was most definitely the Lord's doing for the two little angels of St. Francis Church to be beside each other just as they had been in the hospital.

The Lord always works so mysteriously.

As we were making the arrangements, we suddenly remembered a vision Gino had had a year before Gabriella's death, even before she was sick. His vision had come in the form of a dream. Gino was walking down a cobblestone street behind his sister's home in Italy, where he practically grew up. There was a stone fence there. As he was looking over this fence there passed by very slowly a man on a carriage, and the carriage was carrying a small white casket with angels all around it in gold. Gino ran up to the man on the carriage and asked him who was in the casket. The man turned towards him and said, "Oh, if you only knew!" Not understanding this, he asked again and the man again said, "Oh, if you only knew!" And then the carriage continued on its way.

Back then Gino thought the dream was about his brother-in-law who had been suffering with cancer and was dying. But now we realized the casket the man had in the carriage was Gabriella's. Gino had already seen what was going to happen long before it did. God had given him the gift of knowledge of what was to come, even though he wasn't aware of Gabriella's illness at the time.

Next came the final detail at the mortuary—payment. We needed to pay half of the money then and the balance the next day when we brought Gabriella's clothes and things. We had a trust fund for her but it would cover only half of the total amount we needed for her services and burial. How were we going to come up with the rest of the money we needed? I looked at Gino, and he looked at me and said in Italian, "Don't worry. God will provide."

We went home knowing that by 3 o'clock the next afternoon we needed to come up with the balance. Where were we going to get it? I truly needed to believe that God would provide. We had just lost our daughter. We were still mourning our loss. Why did we need to worry about this, too?

During the rest of the evening the phone continued to ring. Loving friends brought more food than we could ever imagine, enough to feed an army. That night Gino and I lay in bed going over all that had happened to us in the last twenty-four hours. It was too hard to believe. We lay there holding each other and crying, trying to understand it all. We fell asleep in each other's arms, just to wake to another day of preparations for Gabriella's services. Thanks to Sue and Louise, dear friends from Church, we were able to get the rosary and funeral services all together. Without their help we would have been lost.

Before getting started we had gone into prayer. The Holy Spirit filled our house and everybody there. We went up to Gabriella's room to pray, and the Lord was in our midst. As we prayed we felt peace and tranquility throughout the room. While Gino and I were receiving the Lord's blessing our eyes were closed, and I could sense the presence of a large angel embracing us. The warmth and love I felt were very comforting. I decided to keep this to myself, but of course the Lord wanted it differently, for when we were finished praying, all who were in the room said they saw the same angel embracing Gino and me. It surely was a confirmation from the Lord.

It was 3 p.m. All the church and rosary arrangements were made, flowers too, and my sister was going to take Gabriella's clothes to the mortuary. Soon we needed to pay the balance. Nobody but Gino and I seemed to be worrying about the money. (Of course, it was our responsibility.) Then there was a knock at the door; it was a family friend who came by to drop off a gift of money towards the "Gabriella fund." It was $750!

We were only $350 short now, but where were going to get that? The mail had just arrived and I opened it, and in it was a card from a close friend, and with it she had enclosed $350. Yes, the exact amount that we needed to pay Eternal Hills, $1,100 in a matter of minutes! God had provided to the last cent. Oh, how good is the Lord.

That was my final test, to give all up to the Lord, truly and honestly, for He does provide. The most interesting part is that these two people, especially, couldn't have known how desperately we needed the checks they sent us. May God's blessing be upon them always.

Wednesday, late in the afternoon, my sister brought Gabriella's outfit and the accessories we wanted her to be buried with to Eternal Hills. She also had the full balance due in her hand. As the day continued, more and more friends surrounded us with their presents and phone calls. We had more food than a restaurant; we didn't know where to put it all. We were able to feed anybody and everybody. God's blessing was truly upon us, even at a time when much sadness surrounded us. Thursday was just about the same. The phone kept ringing. People continued to come over and comfort us.

That evening was the rosary service. It was held at the church. So many people attended the service. There were people we knew from all over California. As we went into the church and walked up to the altar, there lay our little angel. She was dressed in white and gold and rested there so peacefully, with a lovely smile. How beautiful and precious she was! There were dozens of flower arrangement and white and gold balloons all over. It was the most heavenly sight. Not your normal rosary, but something truly to rejoice about. You could tell that the angels were hard at work.

As we walked toward her coffin we noticed a beautiful oil painting just below it. It was a very special painting, one that had captivated Gabriella the moment she saw it a few weeks before. That was when my cousin Diane asked if we wanted to come to a gathering next door to her house; it was a lady friend of hers who was having prayer meetings on Wednesday nights. I didn't hesitate. I felt the more prayers the better. These ladies had been praying for Gabriella for a long time, and it was right for us to join them. Gino wasn't too sure about it, but at the last moment he decided to go. So off we went, Gino, Diane, Gabriella and myself.

We knocked at the door and the owner of the house welcomed us and led us into the back room, where five or six ladies were busy painting. I remember it so well. It was a scene such as I'd never seen before. These ladies were special, they moved with such grace. Beautiful music surrounded us.

The ladies continued to paint just as though we didn't

exist, until the hostess announced who we were.

"Ladies, Gabriella is here," she said. Simultaneously they dropped their paint brushes, turned toward us, and then gathered around us. I was holding Gabriella in my arms, with her head over my shoulder, and she kept reaching out behind me with her hands and making sounds until finally I turned around to see what she was looking at.

On the floor stood an exquisite oil painting. It captured us all. It was a picture of two little girls surrounded by a field of colorful flowers. One was looking at a butterfly, and the other bending down to look at a flower. Beyond the field, as though one were looking through a tunnel, was what seemed to be the entrance into heaven. It was a very peaceful scene.

Gabriella kept reaching toward the picture as though she knew that place, as though she had been there before. We went on to pray, and the Spirit was present. The ladies were praying in tongues, some sang. It was a memorable evening. Afterward, we thanked everyone and made our way home.

As the weeks passed we kept thinking about the painting. The artist surely must be a godly woman for only someone who has been filled with God's love could paint something so outrageously beautiful. We felt that we needed to have it, so we asked our cousin to find out if it was for sale. Sure enough, it was for sale, but for a large sum of money—$10,000. Well, there was no way we could afford that. Still, we felt that we should have that picture. Gino went to speak with the artist. She told us that painting was her profession and that $10,000 was her price for the picture. We were never able to come to an agreement on a price we could afford and were unable to buy it.

It was that painting that was placed between some flowers below my daughter's coffin on the evening of the rosary. It had made its way to her. I can't begin to describe the beauty of the setting or the delicate perfume of the all the flowers. The painting surely was in the right place; whoever placed it there must have been helped by the angels once again.

CHAPTER TWELVE

A Mass of Angels

For it is written, He shall give his angels charge over you, to keep you...

~Luke 4:10

It was time for the service to begin. So many friends and family. The church was full. The flowers and balloons were bright and cheerful. Gabriella looked lovely. But the most important thing of all was the Spirit that surrounded us with peaceful love; with so much tenderness.

During the service, a lady from our church gathered all the little children around her at the altar and read them a beautiful story about dying. A little boy named Anthony who was listening to the story began to look up above the gathering and make funny faces. I looked up and there sat Gabriella on the ledge above the altar looking down on the children. Anthony was a special child from our church who had undergone many chemotherapy treatments himself. He was also a special angel of God.

To this day, every time I'm in the church I see Gabriella sitting on the ledge up there in her Easter dress dangling her feet, just as I saw her that evening.

It was very difficult to leave Gabriella there that night. Our family members and Gabriella's godparents followed us home. Her godmother Darcy and I went up to Gabriella's room and sat there for several hours, recalling so many wonderful events. We opened up her bag which held all her jewelry and went over each piece. We'd laugh and then we'd cry. It was something we needed to do.

A little later Gino and I went to bed while my sister Elena waited up for her husband and her sister-in-law, Rosemary, who were on their way from Palm Springs. They didn't arrive until around 2 a.m.

On the morning of the funeral, Rosemary told me about a vision she had had the night before. She saw Gabriella sitting on her bed pulling her jewelry out of her bag. She said that Gabriella had a ring on her finger that she kept putting on and taking off. She seemed so happy playing with her jewelry.

Rosemary is blessed with the gift of visions and I realized that what she had seen must have been Gabriella's spirit with Darcy and me the night before looking at her jewelry in Gabriella's room. Rosemary experienced all of it even though she hadn't been there.

When my sister Mary woke up we told her about Rosemary's vision. I showed Rosemary Gabriella's jewelry bag and it was exactly as she had envisioned it. We went on to tell Mary about the ring, which still made no sense to me.

Mary told us she thought she could explain how the ring came to be in the vision. She said that at the rosary service our cousin Alexandria had asked her if she would be hurt if she gave Gabriella the ring that Mary had given to her for Christmas nine years before. She wanted Gabriella to have something special that belonged to her. Mary of course had answered that it would be fine and that she was sure Gabriella would enjoy it.

"Well, she surely did enjoy it," Mary said. "She played with it all night long."

Now it all made sense, including the ring.

At 9 o'clock that morning, a sleek stretch limousine arrived in front of our house. A friend I had grown up with sent it for us and how appropriate it was. A white limo for an angel's celebration. We were to have a "Mass of Angels" to celebrate our daughter's going home to the Lord. That's truly a celebration. When loved ones die we miss the physical part of them, holding them, loving them, enjoying them, but their spiritual part lives forever in the Kingdom of Heaven. We should celebrate for their eternal life in heaven. We had asked friends and family to wear white or ivory, for they were coming to celebrate our daughter's going home. But not black; black shows death. And Gabriella was alive—alive with our Lord and all His angels and saints.

We arrived at the church, and there were people everywhere. Hundreds of friends. As we were going in, the attendant who stood at the side of Gabriella's coffin asked us if we wanted it open or closed. I looked at Gino and said, "She truly looks like an angel. Shouldn't her loved ones see her?"

We proceeded to make our way in and took our places. It was comforting to see so many loving faces. As they began to bring Gabriella's casket up the aisle of the church, a close friend named Becky began to sing "The Wind beneath My Wings." Her lovely voice carried throughout the church. So many were touched.

While Becky sang, a bright ray of light came from a stained glass window and fell upon Gabriella like a beam coming from heaven. The beam lit up her face and Gabriella glowed. When the song was finished, the beam of light was gone. There was a sense of peace and serenity throughout the church and a feeling that we were being touched by God's spirit.

During the service our pastor, priests, and deacons shared very special stories about her that had touched them deeply. We always knew Gabriella was here for a special purpose, and when her mission was completed the way God wanted it He called her home. But we can see that the mission she began continues, even today, as people are still touched by the stories we tell them about our angel Gabriella.

Even though it was time to say good-bye to her shell, it seemed like a dream. It seemed as though she were going to sit right up and join us.

Before the service was over, I read a passage from the book called *Jesus of Mercy*.

I, the Lord, am now here to build a bridge for those whom I have chosen to take My journey, and they will be redeemed.

I shall gather My children of goodness to cross this bridge. No evil will be allowed to cross. Only happiness and peace will come to those who journey with Me.

My little one, I am speaking of a bridge that all My people can cross, if they would allow Me to purify them in My unity. The beauty that blossoms on the other side of this bridge cannot be described. It awaits you, and you will obtain it when you reach the other side.

There are streams and meadows and flowers which always remain in full bloom, because those who dwell and pass through this pasture are pure of heart, fresh and clean of spirit. Once you are on this bridge, no harm can come to you, because no evil is allowed.

The key to finding the path to this bridge is to center on Me, so that I can purify you and lead you. Happy shall those be, who put their trust in Me, for I shall lead them to the green pastures, which await them across this bridge.

It is My bridge to everlasting life. This bridge shall be destroyed after I have gathered all My

children, for no evil shall cross. Go in peace now,
My child.

To this day, I don't know what made me get up and read that. I just knew that it needed to be shared. While I was reading, I felt an inner strength that I know wasn't me. I could feel a presence in me that gave me the courage to read it and I managed to read it all without a tear. I can't explain the power I felt. It wasn't me.

As I sat down I couldn't believe what I had done. It felt so good. It felt as though that was my good-bye to my daughter.

We began to make our way out of the church. I hadn't realized how many people were there, not only family and friends, but my husband's coworkers from Kraft Foods, from San Diego, Los Angeles and Orange County regions. There were children from Luigi's school who knew Gabriella; they were there to give support and love to Luigi.

A friend and coworker of my husband gave him a red rose and said, "Keep this rose to remind you to call me when it is convenient, so I can share with you what happened to me in church during your daughter's service."

Many people were touched in many different ways. Outside the church, they spoke of their experiences and feelings. Seeds were being planted even after Gabriella was gone.

CHAPTER THIRTEEN

The Lord's Therapy

Peace I leave with you, My peace I give unto you; not as the world gives do I give to you. Let not your heart be troubled, neither let it be afraid.

~John 14:27

We were driven to Eternal Hills Mortuary where Gabriella's shell would be buried and waited for Father Doug Regan to arrive to give the closing service. Luigi and his cousin Christina were holding a bird cage with two birds that had been given to Gabriella by her Uncle Carlo. Luigi had chosen to let them fly away after Gabriella died. He wanted them to be free, just as she was free from pain and illness. So when the service was over he and Christina opened the cage door and out they flew. The yellow bird, "Flounder," took off immediately but "Sebastian" chose to hang around the burial grounds. He flew very low, around and around Gabriella's casket, and then decided to land in the hedges right beside the casket.

Our dear friend Tommy chose to stay until Gabriella's shell was lowered and sealed. He later told us that the bird had remained in the hedge until all was over, then flew off and never returned. God works even through the smallest creatures.

We arrived at our house and found that it had been rearranged to receive guests who loved and cared for all of us. My husband's boss and his wife along with a few friends from church prepared a banquet in our kitchen. Kraft Foods delivered a whole truck full of food! Vegetables, fruit, beverages, plates—you name it, it was there! They set it up so beautifully. Only through the grace of God could anything like this happen. Once again He provided more than we needed to feed everyone.

A large group of people showed up. We cried and we laughed, but most of all we celebrated Gabriella's welcome home to our Father in Heaven.

Evening was approaching and there was a little quiet time to reflect on what was really going on. Time to realize that Gabriella was physically gone and we weren't going to see her until we met in heaven. Even though it

was getting late, none of us wanted to sleep. We chose to
continue sitting around the kitchen table, sharing what
was in our hearts.

There were several of us, my husband, two of my sisters, my cousin Candy, my mom, my Aunt Carmela, my
brother-in-law, and my son Luigi. As we were sitting
there my sister Elena began to scream, "Oh, my God! Oh,
my God!" She pointed to an 8 x 10 picture that had been
given to me by a very special lady. It was of a little girl
standing on the pillow at a bay window, looking out at a
field, curling her hair around her fingers. But that's not
what we were seeing. As we stared at the picture, the little
girl became our Lord hanging on the cross with his head
bowed, looking down at a little bald child with a bow on
her head.

As soon as we had all confirmed what we had seen,
the scene changed again. Now our Lord was raising His
hands as though He were guiding someone home, home
toward the light, and as we looked at the picture, the area
of the fields showed a bridge with a river flowing below
it, and over the bridge was a beautiful light. That side of
the picture was much brighter than the rest of the picture.
Where the little girl was lying there was an open Bible

with a red rose resting upon the pages.

It was amazing! The bay window in our living room was exactly like the one in the picture, except that the pillow under the window in the picture was pink and ours is green. We have sheer curtains with tie-backs and pillows on each side of the window, just as in the picture.

Furthermore, Gabriella had pajamas with exactly the same print as those on the child lying at the Lord's feet, and she always wore homemade headbands with flowers, and so did this child. A coincidence? No! I'd say definitely the Lord's doing. He was showing us all the steps of what was happening that night to our daughter. It was unbelievable, but we had all seen the same thing and we knew we all couldn't be going crazy.

We sat there and talked about it for some time. Then we turned to look at the beautiful oil painting that had been placed beneath Gabriella's casket at the Church. It also began to transform in front of our eyes. There, kneeling on a pillow of clouds, with her head bowed, was Gabriella being crowned by two angels. As the golden crown was being placed upon her head, one small hand was folded on top of the other. What an honor! Above her was our blessed Virgin Mother Mary with her arms stretched out, a beam of light shining from her hands. St. Theresa, the saint of all children, was holding a crucifix, with white roses falling from her arms, and next to her was a woman kneeling down, praying to our Lady. We couldn't believe what was happening!

But it was our Lord assuring us all that Gabriella was fine and was being rewarded by His angels for all the good she had done, and that her mission was completed. It was comforting to know that death is not the end, but the beginning of eternal life.

It had been an exciting evening filled with joy and peace. We all had a difficult time sleeping that night, and next morning we all came around the table to see if we could see the same figures we had seen the night before. Sure enough, they were still there. We weren't dreaming, nor were we going crazy!

For the next few weeks we continued to receive phone calls, letters and visits from our friends. But after the visits and the calls slowed down, reality set in. This is what it was going to be like—empty. Not only were our hearts empty, but our house was empty. Empty of Gabriella's smile and her presence. How our hearts ached for her. There was no relief from the pain we felt now that our child was gone. Even though we know where she is, we still miss her tremendously.

I continue to think, what if she had gotten better, what if she hadn't died, how would our life be if she were still with us? So many questions and no answers. Our thoughts can really get carried away. But then I close my eyes and open my heart to see Jesus' face, and turn all the pain, sadness and emptiness over to the Lord. For only He can ease all the pain. Only through Him can we get through each day as it comes. His spirit sends us a sense of peace and serenity that comes over our whole being. No matter what our trials and tribulations are, He's there for all.

On Thanksgiving Day we surprised the family and showed up in Palm Springs at my sister's house for dinner. We really weren't emotionally ready to celebrate a holiday, but we didn't want to be alone either, so we arrived before dinner. There we all sat and thanked the Lord for being our strength and our savior.

It was a little too quiet around the table, and it's not like us to be so quiet. Finally I spoke up and said, "You all seem as though Gabriella never existed. She was with us, and we can talk about it." Then we all expressed our feelings.

They had been afraid to mention her in case it would upset us. But we found that the more we talked about her, the more it made us feel her presence. Our loved ones are to be shared and we should remember all the good and bad we experienced during their time with us. It is definitely the Lord's way of therapy.

Dinner went well until my niece Sabrina began coming up to the table with her toys. Every toy that Gabriella had, Sabrina also had; they always had the same toys. You'd think they were sisters. She kept bringing the toys to the table until someone told her to stop and to put them away. But it wasn't fair to the child. We all have different ways of grieving, and I believe that we need to respect each and everyone's way. No one grieves more than another, nor harder. No one is showing off during their grieving time. We need to respect each other's feelings no matter how different they may be from our own.

In December we received a phone call from our friends in Italy who are like family. They invited us to spend Christmas with them so that we didn't have to decorate and celebrate Christmas the way we always do. The timing was good. Gino and I spoke to Luigi to find out how he felt about spending Christmas with others in our family rather than our loved ones here. He agreed he wasn't in the mood for all the usual family celebration, either. It was just too soon. We made the necessary arrangements for our trip.

I came down the stairs with the last of the luggage as we were leaving our house, and an awful feeling came over me. I began to cry. I felt as though I were leaving Gabriella behind. I shared this with my husband as I stood crying on the stairs with my suitcase in my hand and I'll always remember his words of wisdom.

"Antone," he said, "Gabriella's with us no matter where we go. She'll be with us on the plane and she'll be with us in Italy. She's standing right here waiting for us to go. Remember, she's always with us!"

How true those words were. I do find her in our presence always. We need to remember that when our loved ones leave this earth their spirit is with us always. They are our angels watching over us in all that we do, and their special memories are in our hearts forever. Nothing can take that away from us.

The trip from Los Angeles to Milano took twelve hours. Then we waited in Milano an hour for the flight to Rome only to arrive for a four-hour wait at the Rome air-

THE LORD'S THERAPY ♥ 125

port. Then we flew to Baie, which took another hour. When we finally arrived at our destination we were exhausted, but it was worth all the tiring hours when we saw our family and friends at the airport. We were welcomed with warm kisses and loving arms.

My husband hadn't been in his home country for fifteen years. He was long overdue for a visit. He needed his family during this time.

I knew in my heart that there was a reason for us to go to Italy that Christmas season. I knew Gino and I were there to evangelize what God had done for us. Even though we'd lost our daughter, we'd gained something eternal. And that is God's love, His kingdom. And that's what was behind this trip. We were to show others around us that you can go on; life doesn't have to end when tragedy comes knocking at your door. God turns the worst things into a wonderful blessing. We only have to believe and trust in Him.

Trusting in the Lord isn't the easiest thing to do at all times. We need to be in control, but we need to surrender all to Him and believe the love spoken of in Mark 12:30: *"Love the Lord your God with all your heart and with all your soul and with all your mind and with all your strength."*

During our stay in Italy we were welcomed everywhere we went. But we could tell that it was difficult for some of our family and friends to open up to us. We knew they wanted to talk and share their feelings, but, once again, they weren't sure how we felt about sharing our experience. What they couldn't understand was that it brought us joy to speak about our daughter and our new life with the Lord.

They couldn't understand how it was that we weren't broken down or fragile. After all, we did lose a daughter. But the Lord said these words to His disciples in John 16:20, *"I tell you the truth, you will weep and mourn while the world rejoices, you will grieve, but your grief will turn to joy."* And that is exactly what happened to us. And I pray that it happens to all who are grieving. That their grief turns to joy.

One week during our stay we went to visit my aunt and uncle, who were also Gino's godparents. We shared quite a bit while we were there. One evening, my aunt asked Gino and me to pray the rosary with her. Gino and my aunt said it in Italian while I said it in English. It was a powerful rosary. After praying we began to talk about

Gino's parents who had both died within four months after we were married. My aunt told Gino how sad his father had been because we didn't come to Italy when his mother passed on—how upset he had been about that.

She suggested that it would be a good idea to spend some time at the cemetery, that his father awaited him there. Gino revealed to her that whenever he would dream of his father, his father was always after him, wanting to beat him. He was always angry and never had a nice thing to say to him. But he was willing to go, to honor his parents by visiting the burial grounds, although he was aware that only their shells were there; their spirits are with the Lord in heaven.

While we were in the kitchen sitting around the table, there was a sound across the hall about 8 to 10 feet from where we were sitting. *Comare Maria* got up to see what the noise was, but there was nothing there. When she sat down and continued to talk there was another sound and this time she looked at Gino and said, "*Compare*, did you hear that?" Sure enough, we all had heard it, and we saw the glass French door that separated us from the formal living room move. They got up and went back to the formal living room to check things out. *Comare Maria* checked the front door. It was securely locked and the windows were closed. She then closed the French door. We sat down again.

Shortly after, we saw the door knob on the French door moving. The door opened, and so did the kitchen door, and we felt a cool rush of air. Not a normal rush of air. It was as though something or someone was moving through us. It was no more than three feet high, but the force was strong.

We were speechless, not sure what was happening. It went on for several minutes. *Comare Maria* couldn't believe what she was experiencing, so she got up to go to bed, excusing herself as she quickly left. I stayed for a short time talking with Gino, but he was too wound up to sleep so he stayed up until 3 a.m. The next morning we spoke about it, going over in detail what had happened. We still had no explanation.

To this day we believe that it was a spiritual being. We had been scared, but at the same time we knew it wasn't evil. We knew it was someone's spirit. We thought, maybe Gabriella's, because of the height of the mass of cold air, but we'll never know.

Later that day, Gino drove to the cemetery to pay respect to his parents. He sat there and cried and asked his father to leave him alone, to stop chasing him and hitting him in his dreams, that it needed to come to an end. He needed peace now. He left a picture of Gabriella next to his father and asked him to watch over her.

From that day on, Gino never again had a bad dream about his father. On the contrary, he's dreamt of him in a very happy and loving way; his father has a smile on his face which never was there before.

I believe my father-in-law is happy now because not only did his son visit him, but Gino also gave him his daughter to keep close to his side and to watch over.

Even though we had recently lost our daughter, we managed to enjoy the time we had with family and friends. We visited friends of my husband whom he'd grown up and gone to school with, who are now married with families of their own. We had many happy gatherings.

My sister-in-law said that she didn't know if her brother had lost his head or he had truly come to know the Lord. She had never heard him speak the way he was speaking. There was something visibly different about him, a glow, a brightness. I was reminded of John 3:21:

"But whoever lives by the truth comes into the light so that it may be seen plainly that what he has done has been done through God."

It was now time to say our good-byes. It was hard to leave, but we were ready to go home.

CHAPTER FOURTEEN

The Work of the Spirit

But you will receive power when the Holy Spirit comes on you.

~Acts 1:8

When we got home and things began to settle down again we were able to get our thoughts together. It was important that I answer a letter that was written to us by the producer of Walt Disney's television series, "The Little Mermaid."

A week after we had brought Gabriella home from the hospital, we received a phone call from Kathy Blue, a woman who was with the Child Life Program at Children's Hospital of San Diego. She had grown to love Gabriella and to admire her joyful spirit during our daughter's last hospital stay. Kathy had told Patsy Cameron, a producer at Disney's, how Gabriella sang and

danced to "The Little Mermaid" while undergoing chemotherapy. She told her how she would play the videotape
over and over again, becoming part of the show as she
watched it. It was a way for Gabriella to release some of
her pain. It just happened that Patsy, after being away for
seventeen years, had come back to the hospital to donate
items for the children.

Just at that time, Disney was in the process of developing a character, Ariel's new friend, for "The Little
Mermaid" show. Patsy said that when she heard about
Gabriella and her devotion to the Mermaid she had a
magical feeling; she knew at that moment that Gabriella
was to be Ariel's new friend.

As I had received the letter only a week prior to Gabriella's passing away, I had never answered it. Now was
the time. I wrote back to Patsy and sent her pictures of
Gabriella, one with her hair and one without. I told her
that we would be honored to have a cartoon character re-
sembling our daughter, especially since it would be in
"The Little Mermaid."

Gabriella had loved the Little Mermaid so much that
her wish was to come true. She would sing and dance
with Ariel in the cartoon show. The title of the episode

she was to appear in was called "Wish Upon a Starfish."

In February I went back to work. I needed to do something. I needed to get out and minister to others. Too much had happened too quickly and I knew that the Lord wanted me to share with others the "good news." People needed to be touched and our testimony needed to be heard.

I went back to my favorite line of work, as an artist for Lancome. It was a perfect time to take the offer that was given to me. It was my way to grieve; my way to share. It was very good for me to open up to others. It wasn't as though I went around telling everybody. People who needed to hear what I had to share seemed to appear in my pathway. I could feel it in my heart when the Lord had sent me someone special.

Coworkers and clients were amazed that I was not only working but seemed to be doing so well emotionally, too. I know it is God's grace, His strength that gets me through each and every day.

I believe that my husband and I have received many gifts from God. I know that we are also blessed with the gift of faith.

As time passes we're learning to live one day at a

time. We don't think about tomorrow but live today, for today, and enjoy what God has given us. We praise God for each day that we awaken to, and thank Him every night for that day.

In early June I awoke feeling angry, stressed and anxious after a restless night. All night long my subconscious had been going through, hour by hour, the experience that I had gone through with Gabriella a year before when she had gotten sick. It was a dreadful feeling. I was re-living the whole thing—her waking me up early that morning, the visit to the doctor, the announcement of her illness, everything we went through—it was happening all over again. I didn't know what was going on inside me; I thought I was going crazy.

I prayed that it would be easier this time, that I wouldn't experience this ever again. Was it a way that we need to mourn, a way of healing? I wasn't sure. I only knew that my God was with me and I need not fear. I recalled Proverbs 3:5: *"Trust in the Lord with all your heart and lean not on your understanding. In all your ways acknowledge Him and he will make our paths straight."*

In April I signed up to go on our church women's retreat which was held in the mountains in Idylwild, California. It was my first retreat ever. There were about 200 women attending. The air was crisp and the spirit of God was strong. When we arrived, we began working in any area that needed help. I had the privilege of helping set up an altar. It was quite an experience. The weekend was more than I could ever expect; it was spirit filling, comforting, loving, and most of all, blessing.

On Saturday evening we had an awesome healing service. Many hearts were healed, many pains comforted. That night around 12:30 two lady friends, my mom and I were walking back to our dorms down the dark pathway when I heard from a distance a sound that was hard to make out. It first seemed as though it were the ocean, then it sounded like the wind. I asked if anyone else heard what I was hearing, and sure enough, they all did. It couldn't have been the ocean, for we were up in the mountains. It wasn't windy; there weren't any trees moving.

As we continued to walk, our flashlights shedding light on the dirt pathway before us, the sound became stronger and stronger! I started to feel scared.

The sound crept up slowly behind us at first. Then, all of a sudden a howling force of wind came up. All the trees along the pathway began to dance. As it died down I asked what was going on.

One of the ladies explained that it was the Holy Spirit. Immediately after she said that, the wind began to blow again—stronger than ever! Our clothes were billowing around us, our hair was standing straight up. Diane turned towards the wind and yelled, "Come, Holy Spirit, and fill our lives!" The wind continued to follow us for a while.

That night the wind kept howling, but every time I'd look out our window the trees were as still as could be. I asked my mom about this and she calmly replyed, "Oh, go to sleep. It's the Holy spirit. It can't harm us." But I couldn't sleep. It was such a strange and new experience for me. It was a long time before I was able fall asleep.

When morning finally came, I wondered whether the experience had been real or only a dream. But that day it was the talk of the dorms. We weren't the only ones who had heard the wind all night long. Women with much more experience called it a mighty blessing upon us all. Some kept talking about being fulfilled all night long. So I guess I wasn't going crazy.

There was a rosary being held at 7 a.m. in the chapel for Our Lady. It was for anyone who wanted to be there.

That morning Mom, Rubina and Pat, who shared our dorm, had gone on ahead of me. I told them I wasn't sure if I was going or not. I walked outside our dorm and headed for the area where the chapel was, but it seemed that I kept being pulled back as though I wasn't supposed to go. Finally I gave in to what my heart was telling me. I felt that I was being called up onto a hillside behind our building. It was a beautiful area filled with tall trees of many kinds but mostly pines. However, the area was on the other side of the creek and how was I to get across?

"I know you are calling me, but how am I supposed to cross over this water?" I said to God. I stood there for a short time and said an "Our Father," and then I looked over to my right, and saw a log bridging the creek. I stepped on it gently to make sure it was steady and, as it felt like it wasn't going to go anywhere, I began to cross.

The steep climb in the crisp, mountain air made me a little out of breath. When I reached the top I stood still. So many stupid things were going through my head, like, what if someone attacks me? Nobody knows where I am. Or, what if a snake comes out of all those leaves on the ground?

I continued to pray and asked our Father what He

wanted from me. He had called me up here, and now what was I to do? I knelt down into the leaves on the ground and prayed the "Our Father" and "Hail Mary." I began to feel kind of silly just kneeling there so I closed my eyes and kept silent, to hear God speak to me. A short time later, when I opened my eyes, my sight was blurry. I blinked to try to clear my eyes, but couldn't.

When I finally could see a little more clearly I discovered that I was looking directly between two tall trees, and between them there was a bright white light.

It was very strange. If I looked towards the light, I would see only brightness. When I'd turn towards my left, trying to focus my eyes on something else, my sight was divided—the top part was like a mist of fog and the bottom was clear. It was as though my vision were half and half.

At first I thought the brightness was the sun but then realized it was too low to be the sun. It was 7:30 in the morning and the sun was up higher.

I kept staring at the white light, speaking to God out loud, saying, "I see You are here, dear God. What do you want from me?" I received these words: "The earth is mine, the land is mine, and you are mine." And then the bright white light was gone and my vision was completely clear.

For several minutes I was numb all over and couldn't move. I finally understood what had happened up there on the hill. I thanked God for His words and His love for me and ran down the hill. I couldn't wait to share what had just happened to me. My Father gave me a beautiful message that I've carried with me always. Every time I want to remember the words, it is as though they are written directly in front of my eyes. I'll never forget them.

At the morning service before breakfast I was bubbling over with excitement! The first person I told was Father Doug. He wasn't a bit surprised. He responded with a huge smile, "I told you these were holy grounds. For God is present, and so these grounds are holy!"

He was right. I felt the spirit of God all around us. I recalled Exodus 3:51: ***"Do not come any closer,"*** God said, ***"Take off your sandals, for the place where you are standing is holy ground."***

As our retreat was coming to an end, I knew what I had experienced up on the mountain was very meaningful. I felt I had been chosen for something special. Every time something happens it confirms that I have a lot of work to do for my God, that I'm being called.

As it says in 2 Thessalonians 2:13, *"But we ought always to thank God for you, brothers loved by the Lord, because from the beginning God chose you to be saved through the sanctifying work of the spirit and through belief in the truth."*

CHAPTER FIFTEEN

Gabriella's Visits

And whoever welcomes a little child like this in my name welcomes me.

~Matthew 18:5

There are many times that we know Gabriella has come to visit us. We always feel her presence. She makes sure we know she's here. From the time Gianluca was only about a year and a half, he often told us that Gabriella was in our home, although he had been only seven months old when she passed on— too young to have remembered her. Or so we thought.

Gianluca would be playing in the house when all of a sudden he'd look up toward the stairs and smile. We would ask him, "Who are you smiling at?"

He'd always say, "Look. Gabriella!" and he'd point upstairs. At those times I could feel her watching over us. I could almost see her sitting on the staircase smiling down at us.

One special time that I remember is when my niece Sabrina, who was four years old at the time, spent the weekend. Gino, Sabrina, Gianluca, and I were watching TV in the living room. Sabrina was lying next to me on the carpet ready to fall asleep when suddenly Gianluca began running as though someone were chasing him. He ran around the couch and kept looking over his shoulder. We all looked at each other wondering what is going on. Suddenly, he turned and looked at Gabriella's picture which sits over the fireplace, and asked, "What? What?" Then he started to run again and stopped again and looked over his shoulder and again asked, "What? What?" and then said, "Okay. Okay," and went back to playing.

We were stunned by what had happened. It was as if he were being chased by his sister; it seemed that she had told him something and, as always, Gianluca wouldn't listen. So she made a point of calling him again. Finally, whatever she told him, it was okay. She finally got through to him. Sabrina asked, "*Zi* Anton, who is Gianluca talking to?"

I didn't want to scare the child, so I answered, "Oh, he's just playing around." But I don't think that she was content with what I had told her. She seemed to know it was much more than that.

Many evenings, as Gianluca was sitting between Gino and me on the couch he'd look up and smile. We'd catch what he was doing and knew Gabriella was with us for the evening. What joy it brought us!

Another occasion had to do with my husband and our cousin Davide. Davide, Johnny's brother, was very close to Gabriella. He was here visiting us from Italy. Gino told Davide that many times Gabriella plays upstairs, and she runs from her bedroom to our master bedroom. He thought Gino was crazy, until one afternoon when Gino was at his desk in the garage underneath Gabriella's room, which is now Gianluca's. Davide was out there with Gino when all of a sudden he heard running footsteps from the room above them. He asked Gino if Gianluca was home and Gino told him, "No, that is Gabriella you hear."

They heard the footsteps for the second time, running back and forth, and Davide crept slowly up the stairs to see if he could see anything. To his surprise he found that there was no one there. He was amazed; now it wasn't just something he had heard about—it was real!

Another time, many months later, Gianluca was home

with his father and I was at work. He ran to a corner of our living room, pointed up to our Guardian Angel picture, and asked, "Papa, who is it? Who is it?"

Gino said, "Where, Gianluca? Where?"

Gianluca pointed again and asked, "Who is it? Who is it?"

"Gianluca, is it Gabriella?" Gino asked.

He answered, "No. *Finito* (meaning finished)."

As I came home from work he met me in the garage and pulled me by the hand, leading me into the living room where he had had this experience.

"Mama, who is it? Who is it?" he asked.

"What was going on around here?" I asked Gino.

Gino told me what had happened shortly before I came home. To this day we know it wasn't Gabriella, because Gianluca is familiar with her visits, so it had to be another angel watching over us. Gianluca never showed a sign of being scared but only confused, as though he couldn't recognize the presence of this spiritual being.

I believe that the Lord has given us each an angel to be with us, to watch over us, and to help guide us. I believe it was an angel who appeared that afternoon to Gianluca in our home.

Gabriella along with many other angels surround us. We feel their presence always. There is special comfort in our home.

CHAPTER SIXTEEN

A Dream Come True

The heavens proclaim his righteousness, and all
the people see his glory.

Psalm 97:6

O n October 22, 1993, The Los Angeles Times came out with an article about the new character on the Saturday morning cartoon show, "The Little Mermaid: Wish Upon a Starfish," which explained about Gabriella and how this character came to be. We couldn't wait for the show; Saturday seemed so far away.

We had also received a call from Entertainment Tonight. They wanted to know if they could come over Saturday morning and watch the cartoon with us and ask us questions while we watched the show, and we had agreed to it.

At 6 o'clock on Saturday morning their crew was here

setting up. We watched the show for the first time with them in our living room. We were supposed to answer their questions during the commercials, but that was impossible—everybody was in tears. The cameraman, the reporters, and everybody else in the room. It was a very touching experience.

I'd always wondered what Gabriella would have been like when she was older, and they made that wish come true, too. They had taken Gabriella's picture and through technology they turned her into a 16-year-old mermaid. We were able to see how she would have looked at that age. That's something that would have always bothered me terribly, that I'd never know what she would have looked like.

I was supposed to go to work that day, but the phone started ringing and didn't stop for days. We got calls from every newspaper around and some from out of town. We were interviewed again and again. The local news called saying that their readers were upset to find out too late that the show was on and wanted it replayed.

This went on for several weeks. It was quite an exciting time. We were living for our daughter something that she would have thoroughly enjoyed. I'm sure she enjoyed it from heaven.

In October 1994, much to our surprise, we found out one week before its airing that Disney had decided to make a second episode of the Mermaid with Gabriella's character.

This one was called "Angels' Treasures." It was one year later exactly since the first one had aired. We were excited to find they enjoyed Gabriella's character so much that they decided to make another episode.

The excitement of the show made it easier to mourn Gabriella's one-year anniversary. It didn't seem as painful as it could have been. We thank God for the comfort in our hearts and the peace He has given us. There have been many hard days, and we do feel the loss, but it's been much easier with our Lord at our side. For, again, without Him we could have gone crazy.

CHAPTER SEVENTEEN

Gino's Visions

For it is light that makes everything visible.
~Ephesians 5:14

Recently, Gino had a vision. It all began early one evening when he felt he needed to lie down because of the extreme pain he had been feeling in his lower back. Gino had suffered terribly from lower back pain for a long time, as long as I'd known him. He was told by doctors that he had to live with the pain as there wasn't much that could be done for him. As he fell asleep he began to dream and the dream became a vision.

He found himself in a room where there were two male figures sitting on a wooden bench that was attached to a wall. As he walked into the room he saw a statue of Jesus Christ lying on the floor. Then the two figures disappeared. Gino asked the statue, "What are you doing here?" When he said those words the statue crumbled into thousands of pieces. Out of the crumbled statue stood Jesus. He never spoke but slowly glided back toward the wall and sat on the wooden bench. Gino walked to Him, and as he knelt in front of Him he used his hands to help himself down, resting his hands on Jesus' knees because of his back pain. It was then that he realized that it was Jesus' soul, because he could see through Him. He knew Jesus was alive because he could feel Him, He was solid.

As Gino's head rested on Jesus' knees, he could feel the Lord's hands entering his lower back and then withdrawing.

Then Gino woke up. His back was completely numb and he knew that he had been healed by Christ.

We need to remember continuously that all is done in His time, not ours. God will answer our prayers in His time. To this day Gino has had no pain in his lower back. Praise God!

Since Gino was a child he has had a strong devotion to our Blessed Mother, almost to the point of being jealous of St. Bernadette because of her visions of Our Lady.

When he was blessed with his vision of the Lord Jesus Christ and his healing, he asked in prayer to our Lord to send him his Blessed Mother. And so it was on the night of his birthday on July 3, 1995, after a wonderful spirit-filling birthday party that he went to bed and began to dream, again a dream that became a vision. He found himself in a small theater and there he saw very steep stairs that led up to an open door. He could hear the Hail Mary being sung in a very gentle tone. He could also see a sky full of pastel colors all over the ceiling. He began to walk up the stairs and the higher he went the deeper the colors became, and the louder the Hail Mary, and he could discern that it was a chorus of angels singing her song.

Finally he reached the open door and as he peeked through it he saw nothing but clear blue sky. Yet he could still see the pastel colors that were all around him. Then out of nowhere, like a shooting star, our Blessed Mother came toward him. Instantly she came to a stop about four or five feet away from him. She was incredibly beautiful and had a very gentle smile. She was wearing a pink dress, with a blue cape over her head that fell down to the end of her fingers, and a cloud was at her feet as she stood there looking at him.

Gino wanted to turn and call the world to come to the door and share the vision, but he couldn't. He couldn't take his eyes off of her. All he could do was cry deeply and thank her for being there. It was then that he awoke.

CHAPTER EIGHTEEN

Spiritual Growth

Anyone who believes in the Son of God has this testimony in his heart.

~John 5:10

We have continued to hear the shepherd's call and helped others in their times of need. We need to be aware of those who are around us. We can't take for granted that some-one can do it all on their own. I believe that God sends certain people into our lives for certain reasons. We as followers of Christ need to plant more seeds, to spread the good news to many lost souls. For we are all God's chil-dren and He wants us all to come home to the Kingdom of Heaven.

As He says in Mark 10:14-15: *"Let the little children come to Me, and do not hinder them, for the Kingdom of God belongs to such as these. I tell you the truth, anyone who will not receive the Kingdom of God like a little child will never enter it."*

We need to be more like children. We need to believe and trust in God our Father, for He never wants any harm to come to us. We need to keep our eyes always focused on Him and He'll keep us on the straight path. Remember Mark 10:27: *"All things are possible with God."*

Many times during my day I can look back and see exactly who the Lord had sent my way. Maybe I needed them or maybe they needed me. Either way, we needed each other's words, and that brings me to something the Lord has set on my heart. Church and spirituality. Everybody needs a church. A church to me is a family. When you find a home, and love within that home, then you'll find your church.

Church to me and my family has been St. Francis Church of Vista. The love they've showed for us in the past three years has made my family grow to love our church. Remember, church is God and church is us. God's love together with ours unites us as one, and we need to be united as one to do God's work.

Spirituality is when you are filled with love for the Lord, walking with Him each and every day of your life, being filled with His Holy Spirit, trying to be more like Him, loving your neighbor as yourself. As in Romans 12:11-13: *"Never be lacking in zeal, but keep your spiritual fervor, serving the Lord. Be joyful in hope, patient in affliction, faithful in prayer. Share with God's people who are in need. Practice hospitality."*

This is spirituality. This is God!

CHAPTER NINETEEN

Our Angel Store

Do not forget to entertain strangers, for by so doing some people have entertained angels without knowing it.

~Hebrews 13:2

I'd like to share one other special vision I've had. I have been called to open an angel store. A store where much love and compassion are to be shared. A special store where those who need comforting, who just need someone to hear them out, can learn a little more about God's unconditional love. The Lord made it very clear to me what He wanted in this store.

One morning during my shower, I heard that inner voice again. It said, "Angels Are From Heaven."

I answered, "Yes, angels are from heaven."

But that wasn't what I was being told. Again the voice said, "Angels Are From Heaven." I thought maybe He wanted me to change the title of this book, but I knew that wasn't so. I then went into our living room and began to pray, and as I was in deep meditation it came to me: "You want me to open an angel store." I opened my eyes and looked at all the angels that surrounded me in my house.

Then that inner voice said, "White and gold, and ivory of cleanliness and purity." And the message I was to spread was that angels are not to be worshipped, they are our intercessors and guardians sent from God our Father.

The store was to be warm and welcoming and all who walked in were to feel as though they were coming into a home. And He then showed me Hebrews 13:2: *"Do not forget to entertain strangers, for by so doing some people have entertained angels without knowing it."* That was to become part of our logo for the store.

I was also told that the store was going to be 500 square feet in size and the location was to be in Carlsbad, California. I designed the whole store on paper and showed it to my husband, relating to him all that was told to me. He of course agreed with it all and said that we needed to "walk on water" and keep believing, that if it was God's will, all would be completed as He wants it to be. So we began our new adventure.

And, yes, it has been the Lord's calling. He laid it all before us. From the funds, to the location, to the merchandise, to all that exists.

"Angels Are From Heaven" is a unique angels store that is a little piece of heaven. We do hands-on praying when requested, or when the Lord sets it on our hearts. We're here to comfort those who mourn, to welcome the less fortunate, and most of all, to share our experiences and the goodness of God with others.

The store is truly God's store, and a tribute to a beautiful little angel who touched and changed our lives, along with many others.

I hope that I have been able to help even one heart in trouble through this book. I trust that many will learn to trust in the Lord our God with all their heart, soul and mind. God is good! He awaits each and every one of us with His open arms.

"I am the light of the world. Whoever follows Me will never walk in darkness, but will have the Light of Life." John 8:12.

A Closing Prayer

ather God, I give You thanks and praise for all that You have done, all that You are doing, and all that is yet to come. I pray that those who read this book (Your work) are touched and moved in a special way. And that much healing will take place in each and every heart and soul. And for those who lack in faith, that their faith is strengthened in a mighty way.

I will continue to pray for all the suffering, the sick, the poor, the homeless and the lost sheep in this world.

I thank you, Father, for opening my heart to share these special events in my life with others.

Amen.